EXTRAORDINARY MINDS

The MasterMinds series:

These concise and accessible books present cutting-edge ideas by leading thinkers in a highly readable format, each title a crystallization of a lifetime's work and thought.

Other books in the MasterMinds series include:

Finding Flow by MIHALY CSIKSZENTMIHALYI

After God: The Future of Religion by DON CUPITT

Machine Beauty: Elegance and the Heart of Computing by DAVID GELERNTER

Future contributors include:

STEVEN PINKER

STEWART BRAND

JOHN MADDOX

JOHN SEARLE

SHERRY TURKLE

Praise for Basic Books' Science Masters series:

"This is good publishing. PBS, eat your heart out."
—*Kirkus Reviews*

"Aimed at busy, nonmathematical readers, this precise series evinces solid quality control and begins under highly favorable auspices."
—*A. L. A. Booklist*

"If this standard is maintained, the Science Masters series looks set to play a major role in the responsible popularization of sciences."
—*New Scientist*

EXTRAORDINARY MINDS

PORTRAITS OF EXCEPTIONAL INDIVIDUALS AND AN EXAMINATION OF OUR EXTRAORDINARINESS

HOWARD GARDNER

Basic Books

A Member of Perseus Books, L.L.C.

The Master Minds Series is a global publishing venture consisting of original books written by leading thinkers and published by a worldwide team of publishers assembled by John Brockman. The series was conceived by Anthony Cheetham of Orion Publishing and John Brockman of Brockman Inc., a New York literary agency, and developed in coordination with Basic Books.

The Master Minds name and marks are owned and licensed to the publisher by Brockman Inc.

Published by Basic Books,
A Member of Perseus Books, L.L.C.

Designed by Elliott Beard

Library of Congress Cataloging-in-Publication Data

Gardner, Howard.
    Extraordinary minds / by Howard Gardner. — 1st ed.
      p. cm.
    ISBN 0-465-04515-4 (cloth)
    ISBN 0-465-02125-5 (paper)
    1. Gifted persons. 2. Gifted persons—Case studies.
3. Mozart, Wolfgang Amadeus, 1756–1791. 4. Freud, Sigmund, 1856–1939. 5. Woolf, Virginia, 1882–1941.
6. Gandhi, Mahatma, 1869–1948. I. Title.
BF412.G27   1997
153.9'8—dc21   96-45069

98 99 00 01 ❖/RRD 10 9 8 7 6 5 4 3 2 1

For those extraordinary philanthropists who
support scholarship and education

ⵣCONTENTS

≡PREFACE

I have spent much of the last ten years deeply immersed in the lives of extraordinary individuals—usually, though not invariably, persons I admire. I have read about their lives, studied their works, interviewed persons who knew them and, insofar as possible, sought to infiltrate their magnificent, often mysterious minds in an effort to figure out just how those minds worked.

In this pursuit of extraordinary minds, some of the lessons I have learned are specific: there is no substitute for familiarity with the notebooks of Martha Graham or the sketchbooks of Pablo Picasso. Some lessons are general: a surprisingly large number of features recur across time (Wolfgang Mozart and Igor Stravinsky), across space (Mao Zedong and Franklin Roosevelt), and across domains (Virginia Woolf and Margaret Mead). This book gives me an opportunity to reflect on what I have learned about creativity, intelligence, leadership, and other species of the genus *mind extraordinaire*.

Tempting as it is to synthesize one's earlier thoughts—and make judicious emendations in the process—I undertook this project primarily for two reasons. First, I have concluded that there are four distinct varieties of extraordinary minds. In this book, I seek to explicate the developmental origins and the mature practices of the Master, the Maker, the Introspector, and the Influencer. Second, I am convinced that each of us harbors within ourselves the essential ingredients of these four kinds of minds. Through understanding better the minds of Mozart, Freud, Woolf, and Gandhi, we can not only accomplish more as human beings: we are also more likely to make a meaningful contribution to our society.

Given the nature of this volume, I have kept citations in the text to a minimum. Readers who wish to probe more deeply into the various topics will find ample suggestions in the References section.

For the original invitation to tackle this subject, I thank John Brockman. For editorial stewardship, I thank Susan Rabiner, Linda Carbone, and Brian Desmond. For useful advice and feedback during the research and writing, I thank Mihaly Csikszentmihalyi, William Damon, Robert Kiely, Tanya Luhrmann, and my wife, Ellen Winner. For support of my recent work on creativity, I thank the Hewlett Foundation, the Ross Family Charitable Foundation, and the Louise and Claude Rosenberg Jr. Family Foundation. And for inspiration throughout my writing, I thank a friend and scholar with a truly extraordinary mind, Daniel Carleton Gajdusek.

ONE

Introduction: Toward a Science of Extraordinariness

Phenomena of Extraordinary Minds

Of the billions of human beings who have walked our planet in the last few thousand years, comparatively few have left traces beyond their immediate circle. Among those who are remembered, some are known for unusual courage (Joan of Arc), some for longevity (Rose Kennedy), some for generosity (Andrew Carnegie), some for cruelty (Genghis Khan).

In every age a tiny percentage of individuals stand out by virtue of creative achievements. A few are distinguished because of the prodigiousness and quality of their output: although he died young, Wolfgang Amadeus Mozart created dozens of masterpieces in virtually every existing musical genre. Sometimes they stand out in terms of innovativeness: unknown at age forty, Sigmund Freud succeeded thereafter in creating an influential new domain called psychoanalysis. Sometimes they stand out in terms of insights into their own minds: Virginia Woolf penetrated deeply into her psyche, the experiences of women, and the nature of conscious mental processes. And sometimes they stand out in terms of their abilities to affect others: Mahatma Gandhi, a lawyer from an obscure province in colonial India, crafted and practiced a form of civil disbedience that continues to inspire millions around the world.

Mozart, Freud, Woolf, and Gandhi are very special—so special, indeed, that they here constitute the principal exemplars of Extraordinary Minds. But they are by no means the only exemplars of extraordinariness. Contemporary observers who have looked at the drawings of monkeys wrought by the Chinese girl Wang Yani, the sketches of horses by the autistic girl Nadia, and the architectural drawings by the autistic boy Stephen Wiltshire, for example, are haunted by these evocative creations. We are astounded to learn that Lorenzo di Medici was carrying out a diplomatic mission at age fourteen, that Thomas Jefferson wrote the Declaration of Independence at age twenty-six, and that Alexander the Great had conquered most of the civilized world by the time of his death at age thirty-three. We marvel at the success, against enormous odds, of the Polish-French scientist Marie Curie, the American pioneer of modern dance Martha Graham, the South African political leader Nelson Mandela. And we are incredulous that Goethe finished writing *Faust* at age eighty-two, and that Verdi, Yeats, and Michelangelo were producing some of their greatest works in their old age.

Throughout history most of us have had a love-hate relationship with the extraordinary individuals within our ranks. On the one hand, we have cherished and benefited from their contributions; we name buildings and even whole communities after them, we read (and sometimes write) books about them, we construct our courses and our disciplines around their words and their works.

Yet, at the same time, we entertain considerable misgivings about those who have been endowed with great gifts and those who exert a profound influence on our lives. At first, we are reluctant to recognize their accomplishments, sometimes leaving the creators in obscurity, sometimes rejecting their innovations. Then, after their achievements have been acknowledged, we often search for signs of weakness, feet of clay, reasons to demote them, as if in some sense evening the score. Even as we esteem our heroes, we mortals equally love to denigrate them.

A similar ambivalence surrounds social policy. Most societies have in one way or another recognized the talented in their midst and given them opportunities to realize their potential—setting up special programs either to nurture them or to allow the fittest to survive. In democratic societies, however, we are extremely uncomfortable with the concept of an elite, whether based on merit or on the concept of "to the manner born." In particular, we scorn those with intellectual talent—for example, expending incomparably more resources on those with learning problems than on those with unusual gifts. And we are (with some justification) suspicious of those "worshippers of the canon" who set themselves apart on the grounds that they alone are capable of understanding the great minds of the past.

Even within the ranks of scholars, one encounters contrasting perspectives. Particularly among humanistically oriented scholars—biographers, historians, literary and artistic critics—there is acceptance of certain individuals as extraordinary, and as thereby warranting sustained attention. In years past, studies of the extraordinary—Freud or Marx, Einstein or Darwin, Austen or Dickens—tended to glorify these individuals and to stress their inspirational qualities. More recently, in addition to discomfort with the notion of certain canonical individuals, there has been a correlative emphasis on discovering their frailties, a trend that sometimes culminates in frank "pathographies."

Among natural scientists and behavioral scientists, extraordinary individuals have not occupied comparable research interest. Differences among individuals are not prominent in other species; and most scientists who focus on human beings have been more interested in the patterns that obtain among all of us than in those regularities that might distinguish some individuals from others. Moreover, within cognitive science—the new field of study that focuses particularly on the mind—there has been a strong bias toward assuming that all individuals make use of the same basic mental processes. Let the example be Abraham Lincoln, Marie Curie, or John Doe—all three presumably used the same processes of memory, learning, and behaving; if they exist, differences among them are thought to be at most distinctions of degree, not of kind.

Beyond Caricatured Views of Extraordinary Individuals

It is conceivable that extraordinary individuals lead lives that are so distinctive that no generalizations can emerge from intensive studies of their particular wrinkles. It is also conceivable that, in the end, scientists will find no striking differences betweeen the Charles Darwins and the James Smiths. But it would be presumptuous to reach either conclusion without at least attempting to discover whether there are revealing parallels in the lives of Martha Graham and Mahatma Gandhi, in the personalities of Alexander the Great and Lorenzo di Medici, in the early life circumstances of musical and painting prodigies. Put succinctly, the question of whether there can be a science of extraordinariness remains empirical.

There can be—indeed, there is beginning to be—a science of the extraordinary. Such a science must avoid two equally unpalatable extremes. It cannot pursue the Scylla of "apartness"—the conviction that extraordinary individuals are a species apart, inexplicable by the normal laws of behavior, thought, and action. At the same time, it cannot embrace the Charybdis of "nondistinctiveness"—the belief that extraordinary individuals are indistinguishable in all relevant respects from the rest of us. If there is to be a science of extraordinariness, it must somehow meld these two positions. Extraordinary persons must indeed be constructed out of the same building blocks as the rest of us; but by the time they are formed, they are no longer indistinguishable from the proverbial man (or woman) on the street.

Steering this middle course is not easy. The feats of outstanding individuals can blind us to the accomplishments of individuals who are not widely known. In all probability, for every William Butler Yeats or Marie Curie who makes his or her way into the encyclopedias, there are individuals of equal potential—and perhaps even of significant achievement—who for one reason or another remain obscure. Equally important, all normal human beings can also accomplish feats that, from a Martian perspective, are impressive and difficult to account for: learn one or more languages, recognize hundreds of individuals by face, recall an apparently countless set of events from the past. And with practice, most of us can learn to do things that would once have amazed observers on our own planet: remember long strings of digits; play several musical instruments proficiently; and read a text like this at a speed greater than speech without having to move our lips.

Alas, we have no problem thinking of individuals who have blackened the pages of history—from this century alone, the names Hitler, Stalin, and Mao Zedong leap to mind. These individuals exercise enduring fascination, and they have scarcely been ignored by scholars and journalists. I believe that it is equally—perhaps more—important to understand individuals who have made enduring *positive* contributions to the human condition. These individuals remind us of what humans can achieve and may inspire others to comparable heights in the future. Moreover, I believe that no absolute divide separates the Ordinary from the Extraordinary—we are all human and can be explained by the human sciences. Whatever their genetic endowments, Pablo Picasso and Jane Austen and Nelson Mandela were not born fully formed; they had to develop, minute by minute, day by day, into the remarkable personages that they ultimately became. And so they harbor lessons for us all.

In this book, I undertake three tasks. First and foremost, I seek to explain individuals who are truly exceptional—to discern the patterns that underlie a Newton, a Leonardo, a Jefferson. Second, I search for factors that relate the ordinary to the extraordinary. Such a search entails the recognition of features common to all development, as well as features of extraordinariness that find resonance in the lives of the rest of us. Finally, I look to the lives of extraordinary individuals for specific insights about how others—put bluntly, the rest of us mere mortals—might lead more productive and more satisfying lives.

Before this investigation can be launched, it is important to undertake a few preliminaries. Thus, in the remainder of this introduction, I present some considerations relevant to a "science of the extraordinary," introduce the key building blocks of my analysis, and outline the plan for the rest of the book.

Lines of Investigation

A science of the extraordinary rests on two bases. One is the careful study of extraordinary individuals—at first on a case-by-case basis. We cannot begin to understand extraordinariness unless we know a great deal about the lives and the minds of those individuals who are generally agreed to be special. Such a science must look at individuals within given domains—for example, scientists like Charles Darwin, Albert Einstein, and Marie Curie—to see whether patterns emerge; it must compare these individuals to exemplars from different domains—for example, writers like Virginia Woolf, James Joyce, and Leo Tolstoy—to see whether similar kinds of patterns obtain in quite different domains. In the end, the "scientist of the extraordinary" aims to identify the ways in which all extraordinary individuals are similar (say, in the amount of energy they expend on their work); the ways in which certain extraordinary individuals resemble one another (say, in the fact that writers are far more likely than other creators to have manic-depressive disease in their families); and the ways in which a specific extraordinary person is unique (say, in the solitude and mysticism that pervaded Newton's life).

Various scholars have pioneered this line of study. For example, Howard Gruber focuses on single extraordinary individuals, and Dean Keith Simonton searches for general laws about extraordinariness. I have been most influenced by Mihaly Csikszentmihalyi's "system view" of extraordinariness.

According to this line of analysis, some of it developed in collaboration with David Feldman and me, it is misleading to ask whether specific individuals are creative or extraordinary—as if the answer lay in the brain/mind/personality of the individual herself. Rather, argues Csikszentmihalyi, we must always look to an interaction among three elements: the *individual* herself, with her talents and goals; the particular *domain* or discipline in which the individual has chosen to work; and the *field*—the set of persons and institutions that render judgments (at first tentative, and later more definitive) about the quality of work. We should ask not "Who is extraordinary?" but rather "Where is extraordinariness?" And the answer lies in the dynamic interplay among the three factors.

A few examples. For much of her brief life, Emily Dickinson wrote poetry. She was a person of talent working in a recognized literary domain. Yet, judgment of the quality of her work awaited the posthumous publication of her poems by Mabel Todd and Thomas Wentworth Higginson. Only after the informed "field" of poetry experts had the opportunity to examine Dickinson's work could it render its positive verdict. A similar story can be told about the painter Vincent Van Gogh and the biologist Gregor Mendel—both recognized only years after their deaths. In contrast, Sigmund Freud was an individual of wide gifts and unusual ambition. Yet, for the first half of his career, he moved from one specialized domain of science to another, without ever making much of a mark. Only when Freud moved toward the creation of a new domain—that of psychoanalysis—and eventually stimulated the development of a field that passed judgment on work in that domain did his work come to be recognized as meritorious.

Against this background, I have fashioned my approach to the study of extraordinariness. Following the tradition of Howard Gruber, I begin with careful case studies. Then, going beyond the focus on a single individual, I attempt to amass case studies within and across domains. In that way, I hope to be able to guide the study of the individual (the so-called *idiographic* approach) toward the establishment of laws in the Simonton tradition (the so-called *nomothetic* approach). In this line of investigation, I am strongly influenced by the model of Csikszentmihalyi; that model reminds us that extraordinariness is never the property of a person or a work alone. Only when we consider the person in light of the domain of work, on the one hand, and the field of judges, on the other, are we able to make a reliable judgment of the extraordinariness (or nonextraordinariness) of that individual's contributions.

It is some distance from a method to a science. Students of extraordinariness lack strong models that can be crisply tested. From my vantage point, such work presupposes and builds upon the careful description of individual cases and the creation of taxonomies based on those cases. As scholars opening up a new area, we are engaged in the important Aristotelian or Linnaean task of classification; successful arraying of those data increases the likelihood of a Darwinian synthesis.

The Building Blocks of Extraordinariness

Now that I have introduced the traditions on which my study is built, I turn to a second preliminary: the identification of a set of units, or building blocks, on which one can base the analysis of extraordinariness. To start with, I'd like to posit three primary units or building blocks and one set of processes. Not at all mysterious, the initial units are persons, nonhuman physical objects, and symbolic entities; and the processes are those of human development. From this simple foundation, I aim to construct an edifice sufficient to explain ordinariness, extraordinariness, and the various way stations in between.

First, *persons*. We all are persons: entities that exist in the natural world, have certain appearances, and experience certain feelings, wants, and needs. Persons entertain all manner of relations with one another—they desire one another, fear one another, seek to communicate with one another—and are frustrated when such communication is not effective.

Second, nonhuman physical objects (hereafter, *objects*). We persons are surrounded by a myriad of entities: simple nursery objects like rattles and dolls; complex natural objects like elephants, bumblebees, and evergreen trees; and intricate artificial objects, like hobbyhorses and CD-ROMs. Despite their differing origins and appearances, all these objects operate according to the same physical laws. Technically, human beings are physical objects as well; but it proves useful—and scientifically justifiable—to distinguish between human objects and all other physical objects in the world.

Third, *symbolic entities.* Humans have the peculiar property of liking to create and to make sense of symbols: words, gestures, pictures, numbers, and many other marks that refer to physical and natural objects. (In this peculiarity, more than any other, we differ from nonhuman animals). Sometimes these symbols are material, as in the case of maps; at other times, they are more ethereal, as in the case of spoken language or mathematical operations carried on inside one's head. Sometimes, the symbols stand alone (as in a piece of sculpture by Henry Moore), while at other times they are part of an elaborate system (as in a natural or computer language).

Ultimately, symbols come to be associated with certain adult practices or "domains"—crafts or disciplines that are valued by the culture and that can be mastered through recognized apprenticeships. Thus the domain of law is dependent upon linguistic symbols; mathematics relies on numerical and other abstract symbols; musicians deal with scores that include instructions about expressiveness and dynamics.

Finally, *developmental processes.* It could be the case, as happens with many animals, that human beings are born more or less fully formed. It could also be the case that, while not fully formed, human beings unfold according to a fixed blueprint that remains unaffected by the vagaries of experience.

Neither turns out to be the case. From the moment of conception, the embryo is affected by the physiological conditions of the womb, and, forever after, the particular facts about the particular environment exert a profound effect on what the organism becomes. By the same token, however, the organism (or person) is not simply a blank slate; humans come equipped not only with keen sensory systems and sense-making capacities, but also with strong proclivities to focus on certain experiences, to draw certain inferences, and to pass through certain cognitive, affective, and physiological stages.

In using the term *developmental*, I stress that all individual growth reflects constant and dynamic interaction between an organism, with its internal programs, and the environment, whose constituent properties are never wholly predictable. I stress, further, that these dynamic interactions continue throughout active life, giving shape and meaning to an individual's existence and ultimate accomplishments.

In the following chapters, I trace the development of this person-object-symbol ensemble, in both the ordinary person and the extraordinary person.

Infant

| Direct relations to persons | Direct relations to objects |

Child

Direct relations to person   Direct relations to objects

Initial decoding/encoding of symbol systems
(for example, language, pictorial representations, and so on)
that refer to persons and objects

Adult

Direct relations to persons   Direct relations to objects

| Indirect relations to persons via symbolic entities | Creation of objects in existing symbol systems or newly created ones |

Four Forms of Extraordinariness

As individuals develop, they acquire much direct knowledge about the world of persons—others as well as themselves. As they approach the world of work, they gain comparable expertise with objects and symbols. These skills are brought to bear in various domains, ranging from the disciplines encountered in school, to the requirements of the job or profession that they pursue, to various avocations with which they enrich their lives.

Placing the individual in the center, we can think of the range of skills in terms of this diagram:

Domains				Other Persons
1.				1.
2.	Individual	Individual	Individual	2.
3.	relates	relates	relates	3.
4.	to	to	to	4.
5.	domains	self	other persons	5.
.				.
.				.
N.				N.

As depicted, every individual will develop relations to other persons, to domains of accomplishment, and to his or her self. That commonality, indeed, unites all human beings, independent of the milieu in which they happen to live. However, individuals differ from one another in the extent to which they emphasize one or more of these relationships; and extraordinary individuals differ dramatically from one another, and from ordinary individuals, in the extent to which they highlight a specific relation.

Armed with this conceptual framework, we can approach the four individuals I've elected to feature in this book. Each epitomizes one of four possible relationships of which all of us are capable.

Mozart exemplifies the *Master*. A Master is an individual who gains complete mastery over one or more domains of accomplishment; his or her innovation occurs within established practice. In Mozart's case, his mastery of the musical composition of his time was as complete as can be imagined; one could cite Bach from a somewhat earlier era, or Brahms from a somewhat later era, as other Masters of music. Each domain of accomplishment has its exemplary Masters: we think of George Eliot (Mary Ann Evans) as a master of the nineteenth-century English novel, Rembrandt as a master of seventeenth-century Dutch portraiture.

Freud exemplifies the *Maker*. A Maker may have mastered existing domains, but he or she devotes energies to the creation of a new domain. Freud created the domain of psychoanalysis. We may think of Jackson Pollock as an inventor of the domain of abstract "action painting" and Charles Darwin as the creator of the domain of evolutionary study in biology. From popular culture, individuals such as Charlie Chaplin and John Lennon emerge as Makers (while Ella Fitzgerald is better viewed as a Master).

Woolf exemplifies the *Introspector*. Of primary concern to this individual is an exploration of his or her inner life: daily experiences, potent needs and fears, the operation of consciousness (both that of the particular individual and that of individuals more generally). Woolf left copious traces of her introspections—in her novels, her essays, her diaries, and her letters. Other notable Introspectors of recent times are the novelists Marcel Proust and James Joyce, and diarists such as Anaïs Nin and Witold Gombrowicz.

Gandhi exemplifies the *Influencer*. Such a person has as a primary goal the influencing of other individuals. Gandhi exerted influence through his leadership of various political and social movements, through his powerful personal example, and, less directly, through his evocative autobiographical and exhortatory writings. Political and military leaders influence directly; others influence indirectly, through their writings (Karl Marx) or by convincing leaders to pursue a certain course of action (Machiavelli).

For this study, these four roles constitute the major forms of extraordinariness. It is therefore important to make a number of additional points. To begin with, there are other forms of extraordinariness (for example, the spiritual guru or the moral exemplar); I will consider some of these variants in chapter 8. Second, individuals themselves may constitute examples of more than one form. Indeed, an occasional person like Freud can be cited as an instance of all four forms—for Freud mastered the domain of neurology, "made" the domain of psychoanalysis, introspected with finesse about his own life experiences, and exerted influence over dozens of direct followers and, ultimately, over millions of patients and readers. Third, this way of classifying individuals does not supersede others: in later chapters, for example, I will discuss how the four roles cut across various kinds of creative behavior and various human talents (or intelligences).

Finally, no sharp line divides the forms of extraordinariness. Since every action is to some extent original, no person is exclusively a Master; nor can any Maker proceed without some degree of mastery of existing domains. As further instances of the links among forms: despite their preoccupations with the world of persons, both Introspectors and Influencers also work in domains. Woolf and Joyce are innovators in the domain of writing, just as Gandhi and Mao Zedong are innovators in the domain of politics. It may be useful to think of our four exemplars as arrayed in a circular configuration, with each having ties to the other possible stances:

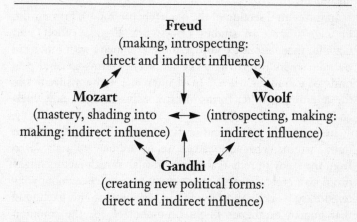

Freud
(making, introspecting:
direct and indirect influence)

Mozart
(mastery, shading into
making: indirect influence)

Woolf
(introspecting, making:
indirect influence)

Gandhi
(creating new political forms:
direct and indirect influence)

The Subtitle and Plan of the Book

About that subtitle: while we are not all extraordinary (or the notion would be meaningless), I invoke the word *our* for two reasons. First, all of us possess in some form the potential to occupy each of the roles: we can all master a domain, vary that domain in a significant way, introspect about ourselves, and influence other persons. In a genuine sense, all our minds consist of these four variants. Second, the extraordinary minds that have emerged in the millennium belong to us. They are "our" minds both in the sense that they have contributed to the life of the broad human community and in the sense that they have been "made" by the evaluations of earlier generations of their respective fields (which include fellow human beings like us).

In the next section of the book, I draw attention to the processes of development in children. In chapter 2, I look at ordinary children, examining the processes that modulate normal development from infancy through adulthood. Then in chapter 3, I direct attention to the phenomena of extraordinary development. I seek to identify those factors that may distinguish certain children from the first, as well as those factors that come to distinguish a child en route to a life of extraordinary accomplishment.

In the central section of the book (chapters 4–7), I review the findings from case studies of Mozart, Freud, Woolf, and Gandhi; throughout I compare these exemplars with other extraordinary individuals as a means of uncovering general patterns of extraordinariness. In chapter 8, I address specifically the question of other forms of extraordinariness in individuals and in the broader society.

In my conclusion, I focus on three issues of growing concern in our world: What lessons can we, as ordinary mortals, learn from the study of remarkable individuals? Which factors might promote a greater degree of creativity or excellence in our contemporary world? And how might we increase the likelihood that human excellence might be mobilized for the common good?

As a guidepost for readers, let me mention three major lessons that emerge from the study:

1: Extraordinary individuals stand out in the extent to which they reflect—often explicitly—on the events of their lives, large as well as small.

2: Extraordinary individuals are distinguished less by their impressive "raw powers" than by their ability to identify their strengths and then to exploit them.

3: Extraordinary individuals fail often and sometimes dramatically. Rather than giving up, however, they are challenged to learn from their setbacks and to convert defeats into opportunities.

I am often asked, "Why this focus on excellence, creativity, extraordinariness?" Sometimes the question is raised for sheer curiosity, while at other times it carries a veiled (or not-so-veiled) indictment of a scholarly preoccupation with the privileged end of the bell curve.

My interest reflects an amalgam of motives. First of all, I believe such individuals—and groups of individuals—are fascinating in their own right and pose problems for frameworks in the human sciences that fail to take them into account. As just one instance, Jean Piaget's justly renowned theory of human cognitive development does not take into account the existence of "single-domain" prodigies, and this single omission calls into question his generalizations about the structure and "stages" of human intellect. Unless we can understand the unusual—be it eccentric, autistic, prodigous, or schizophrenic—our general theories will not be genuinely comprehensive.

Second, I believe that much of the good, and much of the bad, in the world is a result of the thoughts and actions of a few extraordinary individuals. Think of science without Darwin or Einstein, music without Mozart or the Beatles, political life without Napoleon or Mahatma Gandhi. One can recognize the important roles of chance, historical forces, the moment, the social needs of an era, and so on without taking the unnecessary (and, I maintain, fundamentally wrongheaded) step of denying the importance of individuals. Indeed, the very persons who themselves denied the importance of the individual—such as Leo Tolstoy or Karl Marx—have often belied this claim by the tremendous influence of their own work.

Finally, there is a moral undertone to my undertaking. I fully recognize that extraordinariness does not of itself translate into working for the societal good, or even caring about what the good might be. Still, if we are to have a world civilization—and, more particularly, one that strives toward fairness and peaceful-ness—we must understand as much as we can about individuals of unusual promise and achievement. From this understanding may come insight into how better to unite talent and a sense of responsibility.

TWO

Ordinary Development

The Two Great Child Watchers

It may be no accident that the two most famous students of human development, Sigmund Freud and Jean Piaget, focused on complementary aspects of the child. For Freud (1856–1939), a student of personality and emotional development, the central images of life concerned the child's relationship to other human beings: the infant's relationship to his mother; siblings' relationships with one another; and, above all, the dramatic tension between the child and his parents at the time of the Oedipal conflict, when the young boy seeks to possess his mother and to rid himself of the threatening father. (Despite flirtations with an Electra complex, Freud never quite determined how young girls mediate their relationship with their parents.) In treating troubled adults, one looked to triggering events in earlier years. Virginia Woolf's extreme difficulties in relating sexually to men would be traced, in a Freudian analysis, to the early death of her mother, her father's rigidity, and her probable molestation by both of her half-brothers.

Jean Piaget (1896–1980) devoted his research career to the child's cognitive development: the growth of her intellectual powers. Like Freud, Piaget was interested in the universal features of development—the milestones that characterize every child. And for Piaget, the central activity in the development of the young child is her relationship to the world of objects. At first, those objects are completely tangible: the infant playing with her father's beret, the toddler searching for a ball that has been hidden, the young schoolchild shooting marbles. But objects take on more abstract dimensions as a youth deals with nontangible entities like numbers, imagines the trajectory of marbles in her mind, and focuses on the *relations* among actions—for example, the connection between spreading apart (or amassing) a set of marbles and the actual tally of marbles in the new set, as compared to the earlier configuration.

Given the building blocks of our study, interesting resonances occur between the missions of the two great child watchers. Freud was interested in the individuals' relationship to other persons. When it came to physical objects, Freud emphasized the extent to which those objects either symbolized human concerns (for example, the cigar as phallus) or carried traces of the individuals who had created or used them (stuffed teddy bears). "Pure objects" were a rarity, though Freud is supposed to have quipped, "Sometimes a cigar is just a cigar." Piaget was interested explicitly in the individual's relationship to objects, and to the actions that one performs upon objects. He directed little attention to human relationships. When asked about them, he tended either to locate them outside his expertise or to treat the human person as just another "object-to-be-known."

Complementarity is also demonstrated in Piaget and Freud's stances to the world of symbols. Freud regarded the world of symbols—dreams, pictures, narratives—as magnificent vehicles for working out the dramas of the bedroom. Piaget treated symbols as a sophisticated means of portraying actions and the relationships among actions: thus the adolescent could express in logical propositions what the young child had to act out in the physical world. Piaget did concede that certain symbols were "affectively loaded" for the child—for example, those referring to bodily functions—but he felt that this interest was a regressive element and seemed relieved when such forms of symbolization went "underground."

Both scholars focused on a general portrait of human development. This makes their work useful for illuminating the "center" of the bell curve, less germane for the understanding of individuals who are extraordinary in the cognitive sphere. Indeed, both men realized this: Piaget called the creative sphere "a magnificent subject which remains to be explored" (in Gardner, 1993b, p. 6) and Freud said "before creativity, the psychoanalyst must lay down his arms" (1961, p. 117).

While many of their specific claims have been challenged, current analyses of child development still build on the approaches devised by Freud and Piaget. In the remainder of this chapter, taking off from their pioneering work, I present a set of snapshots of the principal milestones in the development of children. In each case, I focus on those aspects of persons, objects, and symbols that characterize *all* children at that point in their growth. Only at the end of the chapter do I turn to features that reliably distinguish young children from one another.

The Mind of the Infant

Neither a blank slate nor William James's "blooming, buzzing confusion," the mind of the infant is already a quite detailed and articulated mental apparatus. Even the three- or four-month-old child has a strong sense of what a physical object is. She expects objects to remain solid, to retain their shape, and to move as single bounded entities; she registers surprise when an object appears to disintegrate or to defy the rules of smooth movement. The infant also has an incipient sense of number: she will treat a display of two elements as having the same number, even when those elements have been rearranged spatially; and she will notice when an element has been added to or taken away from the display.

Infants orient preferentially toward human faces and voices

almost from birth. They are able to recognize their own mothers by sight and sound within a few months of birth. They become upset when the images or sounds of these valued individuals are distorted in some way by a diabolical experimenter. By the end of the first year of life, most infants have established strong bonds of attachment to the important persons in their lives; when separated from these beloved individuals, the infants become upset.

Infants are primed to distinguish the world of persons from that of objects. During the opening months of childhood, infants engage in amazingly nuanced exchanges with their caretakers—smiling, cooing, rocking back and forth in rhythm, all in an effort to maintain close communication. These intimate dialogues have no direct analog in reactions to toys or household objects. To be sure, the infant can develop a strong tie to a cuddly toy animal or a favorite pillow; such intense relations represent an effort to infuse lifelike properties into hitherto nonresponsive entities. By age one, youngsters readily create categories that echo important adult distinctions: they know of prototypical plants, animals, persons, toys, and furniture, and they do not confuse members of different categories with one another.

Finally, infants make many of the same distinctions as do adults. Rather than hearing the spectrum of language as an unbroken stream of sound, they appreciate the same crucial distinctions as do adult speakers of a language—for example, honoring the difference between /buh/ and /puh/, or /duh/ and /tuh/. They also parse the spectrum of colors as do adults—acknowledging the same prototypical instances of colors and drawing the line between red and orange, or blue and green, at about the point that adult viewers do. Infants can remember tonal sequences, recognize when these have been altered in pitch or tempo, distinguish harmonic from dissonant chords, and appreciate the structure of the scale that governs the musics of their environs. And by the end of the first year of life, most children are already capable of "mundane symbolization": they recognize quite a few words in their language, can orient properly when they hear "ma" or "telephone," and utter recognizable words of their own.

The Mind Beyond Infancy:
Child as Symbol User

The world of the one-year-old is dominated by actions upon objects and increasingly fine perceptual distinctions among the persons, objects, and experiences of daily life. He has all our ontological building blocks save one. Young children begin to become radically different from all other animals, including the higher primates, during the succeeding years of life. The principal vehicle for this intellectual spurt is our final building block: the symbol.

As we've noted, symbols are entities—physical entities like marks on a sheet of paper; perceptible entities like words; conceptual entities like the ideas in a dream or the terms in a theory of human development. They refer to, represent, or denote some aspect of life. Marks on a sheet of a paper can refer to a sound (like the letter *A*), a spoken word (like the word *dog*), an object in the world (a picture of a dog), a spatial relation in the world (a map of one's neighborhood), or some idiosyncratic information (a shopping list). A spoken word or phrase can refer to a familiar physical object, a feeling, an experience, or even a new idea (for example, a science dedicated to the study of extraordinary minds). And an idea or image in a dream or theory can refer to just about anything, everything, or nothing.

The explosion of spontaneous interest in symbols, the predilection for using them profusely and immersing oneself in others' use of symbols, proves a uniquely human phenomenon. The domains—the crafts and disciplines of our adult world—are constructed on the basis of symbols; and our capacity to master them, and to invent new systems, also presupposes the symbolic fluency that is launched in the years after infancy.

We all know how quickly young children learn to speak and to express themselves eloquently in language. The one-year-old knows at most a few words; the three-year-old can speak in simple sentences; the five-year-old is quite articulate, having mastered nearly all the grammatical structures of his language, and is already able to tell and appreciate simple stories, jokes, and personal histories. A few five-year-olds can already read and write; the rest are primed to learn to do so, once formal instruction has commenced.

Growth in other symbol systems is virtually as impressive. The one-year-old can sing at most a few tones; the three-year-old can roughly imitate the contours of the songs he hears; the five- or six-year-old American youngster has a vocal capacity that differs little from that of elders in the society (this is, alas, a critique of the vocal backwardness of most adults in our society; singing ability continues to develop in many other lands). One-year-olds can draw odd lines and dots on a page; three-year-olds can represent flowers and suns; five- and six-year-olds can create a well-organized landscape. Similarly amazing growth occurs in other symbol systems, ranging from gesture to dance to pretend play to numbers. Indeed, given a sufficiently rich environment, many a five-year-old is already sensitive to different genres within a symbol system. Such children appreciate the differences among a news story, a mystery story, and a fantasy; and they can even begin to capture the essence of these differences in their own still simple narratives.

It is hardly an exaggeration, then, to say that the five- or six-year-old is a fully symbolic creature—an individual who has a "first-draft mastery" of the major symbolic systems in her culture. The child can "read" and "write" in these systems. The direct knowledge of the world of persons and objects, which had already flowered in the first year or two of life, has now been garlanded with a powerful set of capacities that allow reference to persons and objects through separate symbols (like words) or symbolic systems (like maps).

The Child as a Theorist of Mind

In the 1980s, developmental researchers revisited an old Piaget-ian theme: What do children appreciate about the human mind in general? The answer turns out to be complex. As early as infancy, children have some conception of the human mind, but a long sequence of developments must occur before the child's understanding of mind approximates that of the mature individual.

Consider these milestones. At about eighteen months, children become capable of pretense. They can treat one object as if it were another, and they can join in and laugh when someone else engages in the pretense. At about the age of two or three, children become aware that they and others have distinct beliefs, desires, and fears. They can make inferences about what an individual desires from the decisions that he makes (or does not make). And they can begin to enjoy games like hide and seek.

At about the age of four, a critical juncture is reached. Children become capable of appreciating that other individuals have *representational* minds, minds that can entertain beliefs about the world that may be false. Intriguing experimental proof comes from "false belief" tasks. Children witness a change, say, in an object's location, and also see that another person has *not* been privy to the change. Children are then asked where the person who has not witnessed the movement of the object will *think* it is. Below the age of four, children think that the person knows the true location of the object. After four, children realize that the person thinks the object is in the wrong place, and hence holds a false belief. The child has come to understand the mind as *representing* reality rather than just mirroring it. Only a mind that creates a representation of what is "out there" can create a wrong representation—and so the child comes to appreciate that his own beliefs might sometimes be in error.

To be sure, the development of the child's theory of mind is scarcely complete at age four or five. For example, children at that age are still incapable of appreciating irony—when an individual deliberately states something that is not true in order to form some kind of a social bond with the listener (such as "It is such fun waiting for the boarding annoucement"). Nor can children of this age appreciate more complex forms of deception or literary creation, where—as in a Henry James novel—an individual's beliefs about another individual's beliefs are at issue.

Still, the five-year-old has achieved an important form of understanding. The child can now perceive a person's remarks or creations not simply as a transparent act, but rather as an act with some kind of intention or belief behind it. A person has said something—or rendered something in a certain way—not because it is necessarily true but because the person *believes* it to be true. There are no longer just disembodied symbols; there are minds behind those symbols. This ordinary human capacity eventually paves the way for artistic and scientific creations and interpretations that extend well beyond the ordinary.

The child has now brought together two worlds that have been separate: the world of persons and the world of objects. Some of the objects with which she comes into contact are now seen not simply as entities in themselves but as proxies for the persons who have created them. Personal knowledge can be embodied in an artifact created by—and for—another person. This insight lies at the center of aesthetic encounters. Correlatively, lurking behind other objects, such as those of the natural world, is another kind of mind—the divine force that is assumed to have created these non-manmade objects. This line of thinking undergirds religious and spiritual conceptions. All normal individuals partake of this generative fusion of the person and the object; a few extraordinary individuals can make singular contributions to it.

The *Extraordinary* Ordinary Five-Year-Old Mind

Physicists love to think about the nature of light, and biologists become absorbed in pondering the shapes of living things. As a developmental psychologist, I find it most intriguing to ponder the mind of the five-year-old child.

In so many ways, that mind still seems unformed. After all, the child has just begun school and has yet to encounter scholarly disciplines. He or she has little knowledge of the passions of love, jealousy, or pride—and, unless he is unfortunate, he has not had to face tragedy. The world of work remains mysterious, and it is difficult for the child to think in terms of wide distances or long periods of time, or to imagine life in distant cultures.

At the same time, the child has already traversed considerable intellectual ground. From a relatively "pure" sensorimotor creature, he has evolved to a point where his world is suffused with symbols and symbol systems. These symbol-using capacities allow him to learn about experiences that are unfamiliar and to create communications that make sense to him and that are clear to others as well. And he is already cognizant of a mentalistic world—a world of true and false beliefs, of transparent and hidden intentions, of objects that reflect the hands of other persons or the Hand of an almighty creator.

Perhaps most startlingly, the five-year-old mind reveals how far human beings can advance cognitively without the necessity of direct adult tutelage. The young child parses and interprets his experiences according to his own lights—sometimes, as in the case of prodigies, with amazing speed and precision. We might say that Nature has equipped the child during the first years of life to construct his own understandings of the world: what the world is like as a collection of matter; a host of living creatures; and a conglomeration of ideas, beliefs, and works.

Some of the theories developed by the child are right on target, while others are delightfully egocentric or deceptive. Five-year-olds know a lot about the world of physical objects, what can happen to them and what cannot; they know a lot about the world of human beings, about our good and malevolent aspirations. However, five-year-olds also believe a raft of things that are simply not true: for example, that all motions in the world are created by some kind of invisible agent; that only entities with self-propelled motion are alive; that persons have always been pretty much the way they are today in our culture; that the world is bifurcated into good and bad persons, with the good persons looking like us and the bad persons looking different. Much of education consists of efforts to deconstruct these erroneous conceptions; cognitive scientists have shown how difficult it is to "school" the "unschooled mind."

While already rigid in some beliefs, the five-year-old's world view remains generally flexible and imaginative. The child is not overly burdened by the dominant practices of his culture; he is happy to draw elements the way he wants to, to tell a story in a way he likes, to engage in extensive pretend play. The child follows his own genius. And for this reason, the symbolic products created by young children are typically more flavorful, suggestive, and original than those fashioned by children just a few years older.

The five-year-old stands poised at the pinnacle of possibility. He has accomplished a great deal by virtue of his species membership; he already has a distinctive personality and an idiosyncratic profile of strengths. But he is about to become immersed, forever, in the explicit practices and beliefs of the wider culture. How he combines his natural proclivities with the possibilities and the constraints of the ambient society will determine whether he reaches new heights—and, if so, whether those heights are ones that are currently honored by the society or ones that alert the society, or even humanity as a whole, to fresh possibilities.

Apprenticeship:
The Traditional Route to Expertise

During the first five to seven years of life, the child plays out the program of nature, developing those skills and capacities that are already so preordained that it takes only modest triggering to launch them. The culture asserts itself with full force in the years following early childhood. Some form of education is instituted the world over at about this time. Thereafter, the child's fate is increasingly tied to the options—and the institutions—that exist within that culture.

Every society stipulates certain roles that are needed for survival—procuring and preparing food, for example. Every society of any complexity features a myriad of other roles that make for a fuller life: musician, magician, tailor, builder of shelter, warrior, shaman, medicine man, doctor. Sometimes children acquire these roles simply by observing their own parents (or siblings or close relatives) over the years, and gradually entering into the designated activities at their own rate and pace. But it is not uncommon for children to be placed with other adults who assume formal responsibility for training the requisite skills.

In invoking the term *apprenticeship*, I do not insist that a youngster must become indentured for seven years or pass through a precisely designated regime from novice through journeyman to master. Rather, I refer to the core relationship between a young individual who has been designated to pursue some kind of craft or trade and an adult member of the society who has for some years been practicing in this domain and is considered capable of transmitting its essentials to other persons.

Apprenticeships differ greatly from one another in the formality of the arrangements and the precision of the curriculum. Sometimes, after but a few years of informal observation, a child is capable of assuming the adult role. In other situations, the training takes place for several years and requires numerous steps of indoctrination. There may be much secret lore as well as explicit rites of initiation. The apprenticeship may be self-imposed: Virginia Woolf and Wolfgang Mozart ultimately put themselves through the requisite paces. In any event, after the process has been successfully negotiated, the initiate can become a full-fledged member of the adult community, capable of practicing the skill without supervision, and eventually transmitting the core practices to younger individuals.

Being an adult member of the society is not just a question of knowing how to sail or sew or write; it is also a question of adopting certain beliefs and participating meaningfully in various procedures and rituals. Again, processes of acquisition may vary, but the culture cannot endure unless the next generation of individuals has assimilated its defining creed.

I incorporate all these skills, beliefs, and practices under the general rubric "the acquisition of expertise." The mastery of skills has always been of interest to psychologists; in recent years, courtesy of the computer revolution, it has proved possible to model the key processes involved in attaining a high level of skill.

In general, "information-processing" modelers of skills are demystifiers. In their view, no special abilities or practices are needed to become highly accomplished. Rather, one must simply undergo sufficient drill and practice, with appropriate feedback, in order to become an expert. Perhaps some individuals gain skills more rapidly because they are more intelligent, possess a special intelligence, are more highly motivated, or are fortunate enough to encounter better instructors. But according to the model, any individual who works diligently for a sufficient period of time should be able to become an expert.

Scientists working in this tradition have sought to quantify expertise. It is generally said that it takes about ten years of deliberate practice to become a full-fledged expert; and that experts have about fifty thousand "moves" or schemas at their disposal. Thus, the expert chess player is one who has practiced and improved her game for a decade, and now can carry through tens of thousands of distinctive strategic moves. By analogy, the expert botanist or zoologist has been observing flora or fauna for many years, and is able to invoke thousands of specific details and overall shapes in her attempts to classify the entities of the living world. And the expert performing musician or athlete, following ten years of drill, can fluently perform thousands of different sequences of movements with the appropriate musculature.

Such practice produces behavioral sequences that appear quite marvelous to the uninitiated. Most of us have been dazzled by individuals who can play several chess games simultaneously; identify numerous rare plants or animals at a glance; or sight-read unfamiliar pieces of music or best a tennis opponent who makes unorthodox moves. And few individuals remain unaffected when they behold ordinary but highly practiced individuals who can recall sequences of up to eighty or one hundred digits—this when the average recall of an untrained person is about seven digits! Cognitivists argue that any of us who apply ourselves for several years could attain such expertise. Only practice separates the ordinary from the extraordinary.

Expertise in School

Throughout the world, schools have evolved over the millennia for a few distinctive purposes, including the transmission of civic and moral virtues. But first and foremost, these institutions are charged with training individuals (usually boys) to employ the major notations of their culture: written language and numerical systems. The successful operation of the society depends upon a replenished cohort of individuals who are able easily to read important texts, transcribe information in written form, and carry out those mathematical operations needed for accounting and commercial purposes.

While the mastery of notations remains to this day the principal pedagogical imperative of schools, more complex societies end up highlighting other curricula as well. In the Middle Ages, students studied the trivium (rhetoric, logic, grammar) and the quadrivium (arithmetic, astronomy, music, and geometry). In modern secular society, students study history, chemistry, visual arts, just to mention a few staples. In the best of circumstances, they also learn the ways in which disciplinarians of various stripes approach problems and create products.

Often a society will devise a set of hurdles for the aspiring student. In the nineteenth century, college-bound students had to master two or more classical languages. In the twentieth century, college-bound students have to study higher mathematics and modern foreign languages and perform at a certain level on standardized short-answer or essay tests. Rarely are these behaviors actually required for success in the broader society. Rather, like the masterpiece that all apprentices must eventually produce, they serve as a proxy for high achievement. If a student can log in the hours to learn Greek or to solve differential equations, this feat signifies that she will be able to succeed as a civil servant or an independent practitioner of a profession.

Students as well as apprentices continue to explore the worlds of persons, objects, and symbols but they do so in distinctive ways. Much of school is deliberately decontextualized: one learns about things at a remove. And so the students spend time creating and decoding symbols and notations, which themselves denote concrete entities. In contrast, apprentices work directly with the objects of their craft and with the individuals—the masters—who embody requisite skills. The world of the apprentice may contain symbols, but these are likely to be introduced incidentally in the course of working with physical materials, rather than as substitutes for actual contact with the concrete materials.

Shifts in the personal realm also occur. The apprentice begins with complete dependence upon the master; and he primarily observes individuals who exhibit more skill than he does. Over the course of the apprenticeship, these ratios change, such that the apprentice's skills come to resemble those of the master, and the seasoned apprentice now observes individuals whose skills are less developed than his. In schools, learning is a more private matter, with the primary pedagogical relation obtaining between student and teacher. Personal bonds occur chiefly with peers of similar age, and often skill levels are incidental to these "lateral" interactions.

As the child becomes a youth, personal development centers on issues of identity. The adolescent comes to confront the issues of who she is, what she is likely to become, with whom she is likely to live, how she fits in to her community, and whether she is satisfied with her life options. Issues of identity have become increasingly crucial in our era, where younger individuals no longer do just what their ancestors did and one's options may change (voluntarily or involuntarily) several times during one's life. Such issues touch on an individual's sense of self, relation to other individuals, and skills in carrying out the tasks required for surviving in one's culture. We will encounter these themes as we consider the often heightened "identity crises" of extraordinary individuals.

The Competent Adult

Yet—and here is the crucial point for our inquiry—achieving disciplinary (or scholarly) expertise is not the same as achieving extraordinariness. By argument, expertise is within the grasp of significant sections of the population, providing that the instruction is reasonably good and the students reasonably well motivated. Most of us should be able to become adequate hunters or cooks; a good many of us should be able to understand and employ the basic principles of physics or the analytic moves of the historian. And if we have the happy coincidence of our own intellectual strength and the attentions of a superlative master or instructor, then we may even be able to achieve high levels of performance. We will not do so in the manner of a precocious violinist or chess player or mathematician. Nature has not so willed it. But according to this line of analysis, what these prodigies achieve at an early age most of the rest of us could achieve by the time we reach our maturity.

But, to repeat, expertise is not extraordinariness. Most individuals do not become extraordinary, either because they do not want to or because they and/or the surrounding society lack the means for producing superlative and innovative performances. Nor do most individuals go on to challenge practices and norms: instruction is not designed that way, and most individuals lack the propensity to rebel, to become Makers of domains. Indeed, for most of us, achievement of expertise in at least one area suffices. Such expertise allows us to make a living, to have one or more avocations, to fit in to a community, and to raise our own (or others') children so that they can eventually participate in the continuing society. As for extraordinariness, we can leave that option to others.

Individual Differences

Until now, in the manner of a proper Piagetian or a faithful Freudian, I have largely ignored the differences between human beings. As a scientist, this is a fair ploy: much of importance can be learned by treating a species as a singular entity. To be sure, no scientist denies the differences among human beings; rather, the position is either that these differences are not that important or that, while important, they take a backseat to the determination of human universals.

Sooner or later, however, investigators must confront the differences among human beings. After all, these differences stare us in the face, sometimes even across the breakfast table or in the bedroom. Moreover, a great deal can be learned by focusing on intraspecific variation. Differences in skills, habits, beliefs, and aspirations are sometimes staggering; and it is arguably possible to speak reliably about *the human condition* only after one has investigated its extreme variations.

Even among infants, differences can be observed. The most

salient ones involve temperament. Some infants are quiet, passive, fearful from the first, while others are energetic, active, and resistant to stress. These individual differences prove quite stable; infant fearfulness is discernible years later when children approach new tasks or confront strangers. Especially at the extreme ends of the curve, it proves very difficult to change an individual's temperamental predisposition.

Other telling differences can also be observed in young children. Some differences occur in the speed of development—certain milestones occur far earlier in a few youngsters than in most others. Some infants are able to remember more accurately at an early age, some speak (or understand) more precociously than others, and some score consistently higher on batteries of mental measurement—the early versions of intelligence tests. Differences also emerge in regions of personality—for example, in self-confidence, self-restraint, willingness to take risks, the extent to which one values companionship, independence, or competition.

Most intriguingly, from the perspective of this study, children also differ in their characteristic intellectual strengths. Some children are very precocious in their language, but not in their musical or spatial abilities; other children manifest a correlative early spurt in their drawing or their physical agility but not in their understanding of numbers or their ability to discern the motivations of other persons. Indeed, our own research with preschoolers documents that most children exhibit areas of relative strength as well as areas of discernible weakness (Gardner, 1993c).

The important point is this: one need not wait until middle childhood to ferret out significant differences among youngsters. They stare out at us even in early childhood, they may well have a biological basis, and at least some of them reveal themselves in consequential behaviors even decades after they have been initially identified.

Concluding Snapshots

Among acts of scholarly hubris, a survey of all "ordinary" human development in a single chapter ranks high. Still, such an exercise appears necessary if I am to secure background for an examination of extraordinary development. I undertake this mirror in a generic way in chapter 3 and in terms of more focused portraits in chapters 4–7. As a means of consolidating the points touched on in this chapter, and revisiting the principal themes of the book, I present the following summary diagram:

Periods	Relation to Persons	Relation to Objects	Symbol Systems
Infancy	Attachment to caretaker	Sensorimotor knowledge of physical world	Mundane meanings
Toddlerhood	First peers	Basic physical rules	Play; First use of symbol systems
Ages 5–7	Oedipal drama	Early theories	First-draft knowledge of symbol systems
School Years	Friendships	Domain mastering	Notational mastery
Adolescence	Identity search (self, community); Sexual relations	Vocational choices	Theoretical thought; Hypothetical worlds
Adult	Family, Intimacy, Teaching others	Domain expertise; Option of creativity	Create and transmit symbolic practices

Extraordinary Development

Extraordinary Intelligence: The Standard View

A consensual view about human intelligence is endorsed by psychologists and laypersons alike. According to this standard view, intelligence is a single entity (often dubbed "g," for general intelligence) that is of singular importance within modern society. How intelligent you are is significantly (if not almost wholly) determined by your biological heritage; there is little one can do to change one's God-given, inborn intelligence. Moreover, intelligence has proved to be straightforward enough to be measured by psychologists. In times past, psychologists used clinical interviews or paper-and-pencil instruments; but now intelligence can be approximated through such measures as the time it takes to react to two flashes of light, or even through analysis of patterns of brain waves. And if you are lucky enough to score well in the intelligence sweepstakes, you are likely to do well in life.

Extraordinary Intelligence: The New View

Defying the aforementioned agreement, I contend that the psychometric view of intelligence is anachronistic. Much of what we have learned in the past century from biology, psychology, and anthropology directly contradicts the key claims of the standard view. From biology, we learn that, when it comes to human beings, it is impossible to separate out genetic from environmental factors in any authoritative sense: we simply cannot perform the crucial experiments. In fact, the milieu affects gene expression from the moment of conception.

From psychology, we have learned that human beings possess many different intellectual faculties and that these have considerable independence from one another. Any attempt to isolate a unitary intelligence is fraught with measurement problems; and even so-called pure measures of intelligence are actually contaminated with effects of practice and context.

From anthropology, we have learned that other cultures (like Japan's) make strikingly different assumptions about human learning and motivation. Such cultures have achieved educational success that would be impossible if one were to adhere to the "unchangeable intellect" views of most psychometricians. Indeed, while American and Asian youngsters perform similarly when they enter school, the Asian students have soared far ahead by the time they enter secondary school.

Searching for an alternative perspective, I developed some fifteen years ago a theory of "multiple intelligences." The theory is based on a synthesis of information about human beings, including knowledge of the development of the brain; findings obtained from special populations (such as autistic individuals and prodigies); and identification of abilities and skills that are esteemed in cultures very different from our own, including ones that do not have or do not highly value schools.

Multiple, converging lines of evidence impelled me to propose that human beings have evolved as a species to possess at least seven distinct forms of *intelligence*—defined as the ability to solve problems or fashion products that are valued in at least one cultural setting or community. My initial list of intelligences included linguistic and logical (the two prized in schools and especially in school examinations); spatial (appreciation of large spaces and/or local spatial layouts); musical (capacity to create and perceive musical patterns); bodily kinesthetic (ability to solve problems or create products using the whole body or parts of the body); and two forms of personal intelligence—one oriented toward the understanding of other persons, the other toward an understanding of oneself. Recently, I have enlarged my list to include an eighth form of intelligence: the apprehension of the natural world, as epitomized by skilled hunters or botanists.

While we all possess to some degree the full range of intelligences, individuals differ in the particular profiles of strengths and weaknesses that they exhibit. These differences make life more interesting but they also complicate the job of school; if we all have different kinds of minds, then it is simply inappropriate to teach us all as if our minds were simple variations along a solitary bell curve. Indeed, each of us should instead pay scrupulous attention to what is special in our own minds as well as the minds of the children over whom we have responsibility.

Given my critical view of the standard psychometric theory of human intelligence and my espousal of a multiple intelligences perspective, you may well wonder why I have begun this chapter with a brief review of the standard theory's claims. The reasons are simple. First of all, most of the research on extraordinariness has taken place within the tradition that sees the IQ as all-important. Second, IQ tests do isolate a certain form of intelligence that is valued in our scholastically oriented culture. Third, and most critically, there are youngsters who are indeed extraordinary in light of their high psychometric intelligence, and a good deal is known about these children.

Scholastic Precocity

In the United States, probably more is known about Michael Kearney than about any other canonically "extremely bright" child. Born in 1984, Kearney was a phenomenon from the first.

He began to understand language when he was a few months old, and was speaking in full sentences by the middle of the first year of life. When not yet a year of age, he shocked supermarket shoppers by apparently reading brand names of products on the shelves. He had cracked the phonics code early in the second year of life, and was discovering principles of algebra at the age of three. He had effectively mastered the elementary school curriculum by the time most youngsters enter first grade. At that time, he was doing a year's worth of math in a matter of days. Clearly eager to see how rapidly Michael could navigate his way through the system, Kearney's parents helped him get into the University of South Alabama; he graduated before he reached the age of ten. Graduate schools were reluctant to accept this youngster, even though his performance in college was certainly respectable.

While waiting to determine his next step in the academic ladder, Michael made money and gained sustenance from traveling around the country, visiting with scholars, and appearing on dozens of media outlets. His stated ambition was to be a game-show host, but, alas for Michael, the producers felt that so bright a child would intimidate the contestants. There is little question that we will continue to hear about Michael Kearney, though it is too early to know whether he will remain something of a freak or will eventually make a mark in some recognized (or, less likely, some newly created) domain.

Michael Kearney is an extreme example of a child from the high end of the bell curve. His IQ is clearly in the 200 range—his parents have sometimes claimed it is closer to 300—and he zips through any kind of scholastic material. He absorbs notations and concepts the way other children pick up acorns or snowballs. He is also respectable, though not astonishing, in pursuits like music and chess. Emotionally, he is at best at age level, sometimes appearing like an adult autodidact, sometimes like a spoiled toddler, and more often than not, uncertain which pose he should adopt. (One can certainly empathize with his predicament.)

When one attends to the right tail of the bell curve, it is important to designate just how far out on the distribution is one's focus. I find it useful to distinguish between the "typically bright" and the "exceptionally bright." Lewis Terman's sample of 1,500 high-IQ children growing up in California early in the century focused on individuals who were typically bright—those who could easily skip a grade or two and would be expected to breeze through college. The Terman sample is probably the best-studied in the world, for the subjects have been followed from childhood until the present, when the survivors are generally in their eighties. On almost any measure, the Termites (as they have often been dubbed) do well: they are healthy, reasonably wealthy and accomplished, content with their lives—but the men significantly more so than the women. Most of the women did not have careers, a situation that would be different today.

"Termites" are probably least impressive in terms of creative accomplishments. While a number of them have held distinguished positions and belonged to honorary academic societies, there are few if any highly creative artists or writers, and no scientist of Nobel-prize rank. (Perhaps the most successful scientists in the sample are psychologists, and I can't help wondering to what extent their choice of career was influenced by their early inclusion in this privileged sample.)

High-scoring children have been much studied. One interesting group consists of those who read before school age, often without formal tutelage. Typically, these children note similarities and differences in letter shapes and sounds by the second year of life. They listen to books that are read to them, memorize the texts, and then strive to link the visual patterns they are learning and the words they can recall. By the age of three or four, they are reading fluently; by the time they reach school, they may well be reading books at the level of middle-school children and discussing their contents in a sophisticated manner. Much of these children's elementary education can proceed simply through reading books, provided that this activity is encouraged—and perhaps monitored a bit—by adults. But if such children are not allowed to advance at their own pace, or to join a class of older children, they may well become frustrated by the far slower pace (and mundane interests) of their less precocious agemates.

The relationship between early reading and high psychometric intelligence is worth noting. The connection is not essential—there are early readers who are not otherwise bright (and some of whom may even be brain-damaged); and there are certainly high-testers who read at a normal age or are even delayed in the onset of literacy. Still, our conception of scholastic intelligence is integrally tied to the capacity to master arbitrary notations and to use them speedily and flexibly. Mastery of print is an early way of demonstrating this facility. And so it is not surprising that youngsters with IQs above 170 are twice as likely to read by age four as those whose IQs fall below that level.

The educational psychologist Leta Hollingworth (1942) examined students who were more unusual—one in a hundred thousand, rather than one in a thousand. Children with IQs over 180 are not a happy lot. They are simply too different from others. As a result, they are often misfits, unable to find things in common with their agemates, prone to anxieties and to severe social and emotional problems. Such children are helped significantly when placed in settings with youngsters (of whatever age) who are their intellectual equals. For once, they do not have to hide their academic skills or risk alienating others by revealing what they know, how they think, and how rapidly they assimilate new information.

In *Gifted Children* (1996), Ellen Winner has remarked upon a few other features of the "exceptionally bright": they exhibit notable energy, curiosity, and focus with reference to domains that interest them—in the vernacular, they have a "rage to learn." They are persistent learners; it is often difficult to tear them away from their areas of passion. They are self-propelled and march to their own drummers. Their parents, rather than pushing their children, appear to be pulled along by the sheer momentum of their youngsters' talent or talents.

Questions about Intelligence

Two questions are frequently posed with respect to the bright. The first has to do with the source of their unusual psychometric intelligence. With few exceptions, experts agree that intelligence is significantly under the influence of one's biological parents. If one knows the intelligence of an individual's biological parents, one can typically predict the child's intelligence to a high degree. Even children separated at birth from their biological parents end up with IQs that more closely resemble those of their biological parents than those of their adoptive parents; only when there are extremely different circumstances in the adoptive homes may there be noticeable differences in intelligence between parents and biological offspring. (In other words, from most perspectives, genes prove a more potent contributor to measured intelligence than does environment.)

But many biologists remain leery of a straightforward biological account of intelligence because: (1) we have sampled only a small number of possible human environments; and (2) adopted children are typically brought up by families that are rather similar to the ones into which they were born. Most scientists spurn any discussion of possible racial or ethnic differences in intelligence because the mechanisms that mediate differences in test scores observed within groups cannot be equated with mechanisms that may mediate differences across groups. Put more directly, the reasons African Americans typically score one standard deviation lower than Caucasian Americans may have little or nothing to do with genes, and much to do with latent or overt racism and/or different cultural attitudes, practices, and opportunities.

The second question about intelligence is more crucial for our inquiry: Is it the case that children who are psychometrically bright will be good at learning everything, or do they exhibit areas of strength and weakness? The answer to this question seems straightforward to me: high-IQ children are strong at learning what is featured in school. Accordingly, the more that tasks and skills resemble those that are highlighted in an intelligence test, the better the predictive power of the tests. So, for example, if the intelligence test involves much decoding of linguistic and numerical notational systems, it will predict quite accurately how children will do in the standard subjects in school. If, on the other hand, the test relies on non-notational skills (like solving mazes), or if the school environment is one that focuses on projects rather than on short-answer written tests, then in these cases psychometric intelligence will less accurately predict students' performances in school.

The same line of reasoning obtains to life beyond school. If one wants to predict how an individual will perform at a white-collar desk job, knowledge of IQ is helpful. If, on the other hand, one wants to predict performance in a technical craft or a sales job, then knowledge of IQ is of questionable relevance. I have sometimes suggested, half-seriously, that the IQ test was perfected in France and Great Britain a century ago as a means of selecting individuals who could function as adequate mid-level bureaucrats dispatched to a remote colonial post.

Scholars can come to blows on how general is intelligence. Some—probably the majority—agree with Dr. Samuel Johnson that true genius is "a mind of large general powers, accidentally determined to some particular direction" (quoted in Bate, 1975, p. 252). In this view, if you are good at one thing, you could be good at almost anything. And if you are very good at one thing, so much the better! Others stress the fact that individuals who excel in school may be misfits outside of school, even as individuals who are indifferent scholars often prove very successful at business or in the arts. Certainly, the existence of populations that are notably good at one thing (like idiot savants) or notably poor at one thing (like children with selective learning disabilities) is difficult to square with a view that the intellect is a single entity, under the operation of a single machine, that functions either well or poorly across the board.

In truth, however, one can find evidence in favor of each of these positions. There are occasional individuals—David Feldman terms them "omnibus" prodigies, Ellen Winner calls them "globally gifted"—who seem to be able to learn most things with equal and considerable ease. Many individuals are quite good across a wide range of school topics and remain successful as long as they keep within an environment that bears marked resemblance to school—for example, a clerical office or a lawyer's suite. At the same time, there are certainly individuals who present unequal profiles in school: individuals, say, who are very good in linguistic pursuits but have great difficulties with mathematics or science; and individuals who have a perfect engineering mind but cannot compose a coherent paragraph. And there are individuals—sometimes fabled—who were indifferent students (like Winston Churchill and Thomas Alva Edison) but who certainly "aced" Life 101.

And what of the years after school? Again, signals are mixed. On the one hand, as they age, individuals more closely approximate the IQs of their biological parents—a point for unitary intelligence. On the other hand, individuals perform much better in areas where they continue to practice—a point for different intelligences.

What to make of all this? I say, pay one's respect to school and to IQ tests, but do not let them dictate one's judgment about an individual's worth or potential. In the end, what is important is an individual's actual achievements in the realms of work and personal life. These judgments can and should be made directly, not via the proxy of a test score.

The Contributions of Culture and Experience

Until now, I have adopted the standard psychologist's position that the accomplishments of the young child are due largely to the intellectual powers that she brings to any learning situation. This position has long been popular in Western societies, particularly (if surprisingly) in the United States. Its popularity stems from the provenance of standard psychometric theory and from the reluctance of most adults to dictate the lines of intellectual growth during the first years of life.

Other societies, however, view the matter differently. Among societies influenced by Confucian ideas, like China and Japan, the notion of inborn differences is minimized. What you accomplish is seen primarily as a function of how motivated you and your family are: how hard you work, to what extent you learn from errors, how skilled your teacher or coach is. While the young child may be indulged, such pampering is not at the expense of the acquisition of valued skills and attitudes. Parents and teachers work hard to develop habits of order, discipline, and respect for others (especially knowledgeable elders) in the preschool years. Blatant are the differences between a relatively chaotic Western nursery class and the extremely well regulated Asian counterpart.

There is less consensus in Asian societies about whether scholastic mastery should be targeted in the first years of life. But in the case of art, music, and dance, it is commonly believed that the first years of life are crucial. Therefore it is accepted practice to train children in wielding the paintbrush, executing formal or folk dances, telling a story with poise, or singing in a chorus.

In the contemporary United States, the best-known example of this Asian perspective is the method of teaching violin, called Talent Education or the Suzuki method, after its fabled inventor, the Japanese pedagogue Shinichi Suzuki. When Americans initially saw scores of young Japanese playing the violin as if they were virtuosos, the first reaction was disbelief, the second, that Suzuki had identified the few prodigies in his homeland and rounded them up for an international performance tour.

Neither of these inferences was valid. In fact, Suzuki is an extremely ingenious teacher, who, through decades of experimentation, figured out how to secure wonderful violin performances out of perfectly ordinary youngsters. The method, much written about, includes the early establishment of a bond between the mother and the instrument; brief daily practice sessions involving mother and child; ample opportunities to perform with and observe other children, especially those who exhibit different levels of competence; selection of a repertoire that is appealing to listen to and easy to finger; ample exposure to tapes that embody exemplary performance; and a milieu fostering love of music.

The Suzuki method turns out to be just the tip of an East Asian iceberg. Many programs throughout the Asian lands train youngsters to perform at a high level in an art form, a music form, or some athletic or other skill activity. Taking proper note, Western coaches and parents have instituted similar programs spanning the gamut from early swimming to early reading to early math. Sometimes (and these are the happier occasions) the training is part of a rich milieu involving family enjoyment; at other times, one has the feeling that one is observing trained seals, who are having as much (read as little) fun as their aquatic counterparts. Of course, this split is not present only in the United States; early educational interventions the world over can exhibit either accent.

In between the unstructured indulgence of much Western education and the overly prescribed regimen of a Suzuki training or a Chinese calligraphic class, attractive options exist. I think, for example, of the many American youngsters who achieve virtually an expert's knowledge of dinosaurs, often aided by books, toys, and occasional trips to a natural history museum, but with little need for prompting or rewards from adults; or of the many youngsters who learn to use computers through a combination of conversation with peers seated at a terminal and enlightened trial and error; or of the Northern Italian community of Reggio Emilia, where young schoolchildren focus for months on topics that interest them and, under the guidance of skilled teachers, end up creating beautiful art objects and arresting performances.

The debate about the relative importance of "talent" and "training" has recently reemerged in academic psychology circles. The psychologist Anders Ericsson and his colleagues have amassed impressive evidence that—in domains ranging from musical performance to the memorization of digits—skilled practitioners differ from one another chiefly in the number of hours of "deliberate practice" in which they have repeatedly engaged. But counter to his hope, Ericsson has not slain the dragon of talent. Skeptics (including me) point out that only those with talent are likely to practice for thousands of hours, and that sheer practice is less likely to be effective in highly cognitive domains such as mathematics, chess, and musical composition.

Five-Year-Old Domain Prodigies

So far we have seen that unusual levels of performance can come from two quite different sources: children of high psychometric intelligence, who have been allowed to advance at their own rate in a scholastic environment; and children who may themselves not be remarkable but who are the beneficiaries of a pedagogical method that either develops specific skills (such as violin playing) or provides a very rich set of experiences (as in the regular cultivation of crafts at the Reggio Emilia schools).

Until now, I have left unsurveyed those children who are most likely to become extraordinary adults—in the sense that they end up affecting a domain or a population. These are individuals who, as early as five or so, distinguish themselves because of their accomplishment in a specific domain.

Classically, there have been three domains of early precocity: chess, musical performance, and mathematical understanding. One finds prodigies in each of these domains—youngsters who are already performing at the level of competent adults. Typically, such youngsters display an early interest in the game of chess, in playing an instrument, or in calculating and playing numerical games. These interests are encouraged by adults, but most parents report that the child seems to be "possessed" by his interest, so much so that he wants to spend hours each day involved with chess moves, multiplication problems, or practicing (often with variations) a particular song on his instrument.

It is not surprising that precocity occurs in these specific domains. They are relatively circumscribed, each with its set of symbols and governing rules. One becomes skilled by learning rules and following them assiduously. No knowledge is needed about subtler aspects of experience, no necessity to undergo certain personal forms of discovery. (This is probably why precocity in realms like literature, political leadership, or morality is far less common.) It is possible that these three forms of precocity all exploit a central talent with numerical or spatial patterns—such is the line of argument that believers in a "general intellect" perspective would endorse. But before acccepting this hypothesis, remember that most youngsters are precocious in one of these domains, not all three; and that while there is a numerical component to each, spatial abilities are far more important in chess, and musical sensitivity and physical dexterity are of the essence in musical performance.

Our prototyptical prodigies, then, are the youthful Yo-Yo Ma or Yehudi Menuhin, two string instrumentalists; Norbert Wiener and Carl Friedrich Gauss, two precocious mathematicians; and Sammy Reshevsky and Bobby Fischer, two chess prodigies. These individuals are all presumably of high psychometric intelligence, but especially with respect to musicians and chess players, there is no reason to think that they would necessarily belong to the extraordinarily bright group.

In recent years, there has been a spurt in the incidence of female prodigies, such as the Polgar sisters, the chess champions; and string players like Midori and Sara Chang. Also, prodigies have begun to be noted in other domains, such as Wang Yani, a precocious master of Chinese ink and brush painting; and Alexandra Nechita, an American who has been compared to Picasso. Before one assumes that only certain domains, or only boys, can assume prodigious status, it is crucial to see which activities are valued by a society and which members of that society are encouraged (or discouraged) from that activity. For example, Yo-Yo Ma's sister, highly talented in music, was discouraged from pursuing the same career as her prodigiously talented brother.

It must be said, succinctly but firmly, that while such prodigiousness begins with individual talent, it cannot come to fruition without a good deal of support. Studies of high-achieving youngsters document the enormous amount of support given by parents, other family members, teachers, and, not infrequently, others in the community. No one, no matter how talented, can forge ahead alone. However, the support is unlikely to achieve much in the absence of native intelligence(s) and a "rage to learn."

Unfortunately, little is known about the early antecedents of our four kinds of extraordinary minds. Precocity seems to occur principally in domains that stress objects and symbols; either young children are not precocious in the realm of persons, or we do not yet know the signs of such gifts. Because domains have not yet coalesced, the distinction between Maker and Master remains somewhat theoretical in the case of most children. However, it seems plausible to hypothesize that children are more likely to become Makers when they have a temperament that welcomes tension, when they are later-born (and hence more rebellious), and when they choose to work in a domain that has already been intensively explored in its current guise. Finally, the relation between the child's intelligences and the domains proves important. Because of the close fit between mind and matter, a prodigy is likely to move toward Mastering a domain; in cases where intelligences are at variance with common domain practices, there may be a shift toward Making.

The Exceptional Extraordinary

In at least one respect, it is not that difficult to account for a Wang Yani or a Yehudi Menuhin. After all, it is reasonable to assume that these two individuals were quite bright, with many potentials; their move toward specific domains was crystallized in part by an early interest, in part by a highly supportive environment.

Far more challenging to the analyst are those occasional individuals who are extremely impaired in most domains, save a single one. These youngsters are often autistic—impaired individuals whose communicative capacities (in any established symbol system) range from meager to nonexistent. Despite such handicaps, the Rumanian-born Nadia was able from her preschool years to make pencil drawings of horses and humans that were highly skilled and expressive; Stephen Wiltshire was able to render expert architectural drawings, both from observation and from his imagination; John and Michael, the pair of autistic twins studied by Oliver Sacks, were able to calculate large sums and to identify the day of the week of any date from the last century; and, despite blindness and retardation, Leslie Lemke taught himself to play the piano with great skill, often learning complex pieces following a single hearing.

Clearly, in such cases, one is not confronting an intact intellect. Nor, if we can believe the testimony of those closest to the case, are we dealing with instances where a parent or therapist has zealously trained one spared skill. Indeed, in the case of the young visual artist Nadia, her talent was discovered by a clinician who was examining her—Nadia's mother was not even aware that her daughter had been drawing in an unusual way. Rather, we are confronting a single preserved intellectual capacity, reflecting an intelligence or a set of intelligences that happens to map with astonishing precision onto a domain to which the child has been exposed in his or her culture. Once this link has been made, the child needs scant tutelage; exploration of the regularities within the domain suffices to produce performances of dazzling quality. Indeed, it has been suggested that autistic individuals may even excel in certain domains precisely because they are not hamstrung by more conventional ways of expressing themselves or communicating to others.

We are all aware of individuals of seemingly ordinary background and capacities who go on to accomplish astounding feats—oft-cited instances range from Charles Darwin, an indifferent student, to Harry Truman, a certified failure at age forty. Researchers of the extraordinary can chronicle many examples of individuals who showed enormous promise (like Norbert Wiener's contemporary William James Sidis) but whose careers crashed in later life. And for every Stephen Wiltshire or Temple Grandin who can convert an autistic talent into a living, there are many others, like Nadia, who remain institutionalized and indifferent to the admiring world. Finally, to complete the pattern, there are the rare individuals who stand out equally in terms of their initial precocity and their ultimate creative achievements—with Pablo Picasso and Wolfgang Mozart probably the outstanding examples in recent Western history.

Five Experiences a Day

I am sometimes asked why I do not just accept the power of an individual's biological heritage and let it go at that. To counter this temptation, I administer the following thought experiment, called Five Experiences a Day.

Take any two persons, any two organisms, matched as much as one could envision. One can even, in the extreme, imagine identical twins who were separated not at birth but at conception. Now imagine that one person, called B (for benign), undergoes five positive experiences a day—these can be physically, emotionally, or cognitively positive. Imagine that the second person, called M (for malign) encounters five negative experiences a day—again, these can involve the mind, the heart, the body. By the time of birth, nine months later, B will have had over 1,300 positive experiences, while M will have had over 1,300 negative experiences—for a total disparity of 2,600 experiences.

Now advance the calendar five more years, until the Western age of five. One can add 9,000 additional positive experiences for B and 9,000 additional negative experiences for M—the total difference in experiences being 10,300+ in one direction for B, 10,300- in the less happy direction for M. Can one really expect these individuals—with a disparity of 20,600 experiences—to be anything but radically different from each other? Indeed, even if they were identical twins, B is likely to feel positively about himself, to have had a chance to acquire some skills, and to be motivated to do more, while M is likely to be malnourished, unhappy, unmotivated, well on the road to being a failure in his own eyes and in those of the surrounding community.

Perhaps this experience is not repeated in exactly this form too often, and yet it is uncontroversial that some individuals lead lives that are more like B's and that all too many individuals undergo experiences that more closely resemble M's. The five-year-old mind may in some ways remain unformed, but the five-year-old person is quite well formed in many respects. If we want to understand how some individuals manage to become exceptional in a positive sense by the age of five, we will need to know more about brain and biology; but we will equally need to know more about the experiences that pluck a few of us out of the crowd and give us the opportunity to become a special kind of person.

And On to Four Exemplary Minds . . .

It is easy to recognize individuals who stand out in terms of their high psychometric intelligence or their skill in a recognized area of talent, like chess or music or painting. However, there may well be youngsters who are equally precocious in other domains, ranging from the understanding of others to the understanding of self, from literary sensitivity to inventive genius. Once we have a better understanding of how these abilities develop throughout childhood, we may be able to broaden our portrait to include these varieties of giftedness. It is also important to note that ultimate achievements are not always foretold in childhood. Some individuals are late bloomers; skill in some domains may not emerge until adolescence or even later; and otherwise ordinary individuals may be stimulated to great achievements through the intervention of circumstances, encouraging as well as bitter. Having a blissfully happy childhood may be understimulating, even as a series of tragedies can cripple even the most promising youth. Of our four extraordinary subjects, only Mozart's particular gifts were evident from an early age.

Against the background of normal development that characterizes most individuals, we have focused here on those factors that make for an extraordinary childhood. Precocity is most likely to come about if an individual has a high psychometric intelligence, or a special gift in some other variety of intelligence, *and* the proper kind of nurturance from family and the surrounding culture. One Western individual has represented the co-occurrence of these factors with unparalleled vividness, and so it is appropriate to begin our investigation of extraordinary minds with a consideration of Mozart.

FOUR

Master:
The Case of Mozart

Lessons Well Learned

In 1785, the twenty-nine-year-old Wolfgang Amadeus Mozart completed a set of six string quartets (K. 387, 421/417b, 428/421b, 458, 464, 465). In itself this fact is unremarkable. Mozart was a prolific composer, and he often composed sets of pieces for a single instrument or an ensemble. But Mozart's labor on these pieces over a three-year period was unprecedented. He had carefully studied the compositional approach of his older contemporary Franz Joseph Haydn. He was challenged—and inspired—by Haydn's skill at counterpoint and chromaticism; his ability to bring out the genius of each instrument as it contributed to the articulation of a theme; the way he structured movements and varied moods. In contrast to his usual fluid mode of composition, Mozart pored over numerous drafts and even made changes in the printed version. Calling these compositions "the fruit of a long and laborious effort" Mozart prepared a formal dedication:

> To my dear friend Haydn: A father, having resolved to send his sons into the great world, finds it advisable to entrust them to the protection and guidance of a highly celebrated man, the more so since this man, by a stroke of luck, is his best friend. Here, then, celebrated man, and my dearest friend, are my six sons . . . your approval encourages me more than anyone else. [quoted in Robbins-Landon, 1988, p. 23]

Though they met only a few times, the men realized a special bond that united them. The supremely confident Mozart understood that Haydn was perhaps the only contemporary from whom he could learn as an adult. Haydn, nearly a quarter-century older than Mozart, prized his own abilities. Still, he recognized the unique achievements of his younger soulmate. Indeed, when he had the opportunity to speak to Mozart's father, Leopold, Haydn famously declared: "Before God and as an honest man, I tell you that your son is the greatest composer known to me either in person or by name. He has taste, and, what is more, the most profound knowledge of composition" (quoted in Solomon, 1995, p. 314).

From his earliest days, as part of his musical apprenticeship, Mozart had always attended to compositional models. In his previous encounters, he had been able to assimilate style and technique in a virtually seamless manner; but the string quartets called for an attention to structure, detail, and compositional technique that did not come spontaneously to him. Instead, like an attentive student at the feet of a master teacher, Mozart had to dissect the models, identify their crucial components, and revise drafts repeatedly before affirming that the pieces were up to the standard of his admired master.

There is another, equally important aspect to the Haydn-Mozart relationship. From the time of his birth, Mozart's life had been dominated by his father. A talented violinist, teacher, and minor composer himself, Leopold had early recognized the genius of his son and had devoted himself unstintingly to the promotion of young Wolfgang's career. (Music historians debate whether Leopold's championing had a touch of selflessness, or whether this investment in his son's career was done for the father's own glory.) By the early 1780s Mozart wanted desperately to break from his father and become his own man, personally as well as musically. What better way than to substitute Haydn as a redoubtable father figure? While Mozart as dedicator may have used the father/son analogy as a literary device, it is indisputable that breaking away from a dominating father was his chief motive as he neared his thirtieth birthday.

Genius Unadorned

Much bandied about these days, the word *genius* should properly be saved for people who stand out even among the extraordinary—those rare individuals whose shadows dominate the history of successive eras. By any definition, Mozart qualifies as a genius. He is most properly classed with a few other outstanding composers—Bach from the preceding generation, Beethoven from the succeeding generation—and with a few other seminal artists: Shakespeare and Goethe among writers, Rembrandt and Picasso among painters, Michelangelo and Rodin among sculptors.

Some members of this rarefied company are "particularistic" geniuses. Among composers, Beethoven and Wagner possessed strong personalities and philosophies, which suffused their music; one could make similar statements about the writings of Victor Hugo or the paintings of Francisco José de Goya.

Mozart exemplifies the "universal" genius. His own personality does not emerge in its idiosyncratic way in his works. We know Mozart as a person no better from the tragic strains of his 40th (G minor) symphony than from the triumphant bars of his 41st (Jupiter) symphony. Rather, Mozart was able to place himself completely at the service of the genres and themes with which he worked—a statement that one could also make about Shakespeare or Goethe. The poet John Keats described the capacity to submerge oneself in one's artistic materials:

As to the poetical character, itself, it is not itself—it has not self—it is everything and nothing—it has no character—it enjoys light and shadow—it lives in gusto, be it foul or fair, high or low, rich or poor, mean or elevated. . . . A poet is the most unpoetical thing in existence because he has no identity—he is continually in form—and filling some other body. . . . When I am in a room with people if I ever am free from speculating on creations of my own brain, then not myself goes home to myself, but the identity of everyone in the room begins to press upon me [so] that I am in a very little time annihilated—not only among men: it would be same in a Nursery of children. [quoted in Bate, 1963, pp. 260–61]

This rough differentiation within the species of genius proves useful for our purposes. By and large, a Master—like Mozart—has as his goals the complete mastery of the genres of his time and the desire to create works of the highest quality within those genres. By inclination a classicist, he realizes himself by means of the languages that are available. In contrast, the Maker—like Beethoven—ultimately throws off the dominant genres and domains of his era in order to create a new form of expression. The voice of the Maker is far more likely to be heard in its particular accents and with its peculiar prejudices. A romantic, the Maker creates the idiom that allows him to express his own person authentically.

In creating the quartets in Haydn's image and dedicating that set to him, Mozart was confirming his own place in a continuing classical order. Paradoxically, by his participation in, and total mastery of, this tradition, he was laying the groundwork for the emergence of the new approaches "made" by Beethoven and his Romantic successors.

Wunderkind

Mozart was certainly a child of ability in several spheres: he liked numbers, picked up languages readily, and enjoyed the games and jokes of childhood—in fact, continuing to pursue such tomfoolery throughout his adult years. But beyond question, Mozart's musical accomplishments totally outstripped his achievements in any other domain, and indeed may have eclipsed those of any other human being in the realm of the arts.

Here are the agreed-upon facts. Mozart began to play the piano at the age of three. By four he was already learning pieces readily. At the same time, he observed others playing the violin and was able to teach himself the rudiments without formal tutelage. By the age of five he had begun to compose, and by seven he was composing regularly. Pieces preserved from his earliest years are charming, and pieces from his adolescent years are already ambitious in scope and achievement.

With the rest of his family (including his talented sister, Nannerl) in tow, Mozart began to tour Europe when he was seven and spent much of the rest of his childhood giving performances in the leading concert halls and salons of Europe. In addition to performing his own and others' pieces, he accomplished legendary musical feats. For example, he listened but once to Gregorio Allegri's *Miserere*, a highly complex religious composition that musicians were forbidden to remove from a sacred chapel, and subsequently transcribed the whole piece from memory virtually without error.

The most important chapter of Mozart's childhood was the development of his compositional skills. Probably stimulated by his father, he began to create pieces of music at an age when most children are scarcely able to speak in full sentences. At first, his compositions were clearly influenced by Leopold, who not only transcribed them but probably edited them significantly. But by the time he was seven or eight, young Mozart was already composing on his own a steady stream of pieces in a range of genres. It is staggering to contemplate his prolificness: at age ten, for instance, he arranged concerti and also composed an oratorio, a piece of Passion music, and a Latin comedy for the university; at twelve he wrote an opera, a new mass, shorter sacred works, several sets of minuets for dancing, and three substantial orchestral serenades (Grove, 1980, pp. 682–83). At age fourteen he casually writes: "In the meantime, I have composed four Italian symphonies, to say nothing of arias, of which I must have composed at least five or six and also a motet" (quoted in Blom, 1956, p. 16). His biographer Turner computes twenty-six pieces in a six-month period, including seven symphonies (1956, p. 128).

Mozart's travels exposed him to the music of many composers. Intriguingly, he was most strongly influenced by members of the premier musical families of the century—Joseph Haydn's brother Michael and Johann Sebastian Bach's son Johann Christian. Mozart's compositions of the period are highly reminiscent of those created by these models; indeed, it is often difficult to identify the composer of these pieces. His many letters home reveal the steady growth of his musical consciousness and contain penetrating reflections about performances, performers, and the processes of composition.

Mozart's pieces gradually took on more of an individual character. While the pieces composed at ages seven or eight are simply plausible representatives of the classical style, the pieces between the ages of twelve and fifteen are already identifiable in particular phrases as "Mozartisch." Turner goes so far as to claim that by the age of ten, Mozart was "an accomplished master of the contemporary craft of composition equal to any living composer of his time" (p. 61). And by the age of fifteen—when Mozart had been composing for a decade—his pieces attain a quality that earned them a place in the permanent repertory.

Mozart exhibits, as do few other human beings in history, the incredible synergistic confluence of disparate factors and events—what David Feldman has called "co-incidence" in the childhood of the prodigy. Mozart lived at a time when classical music was prized and when it was possible for a talented young performer to earn money in the courts of Europe; he had a father who was a skilled (if somewhat pedantic) music teacher, and who was willing to devote his life and career to the nurturance of his "gift from God"; he had incredible musical gifts, which certainly included the ability to remember just about everything he heard and to figure out how to realize it on a keyboard (and other instruments); he had the skill, the personality, the will, indeed the rage to transcend mere performance and to want to create works of music of his own (and, soon, on his own). Indeed, from child-hood, he was totally dedicated to musical composition; he lived to compose and desired little else—"my sole delight and passion," he declared (quoted in Blom, p. 45).

It should be pointed out that the line between performance and creation was less sharp in Mozart's day than in our own. Yet this by no means explains his exceptional musical efflorescence, with pieces appearing on an almost daily basis when young, and with entire symphonies and operas being created at breakneck speed even when he was most disconsolate as an adult.

Prodigies and Creators

For Mozart, everything went completely right as a young child. The brain, the mind, and the spirit worked together with the family and the wider cultural context to ensure a child who was music incarnate. Appreciation of this confluence can bring the Miraculous a bit closer to the realm of Reality—after all, there were no complicating factors. Yet the very co-incidence of factors that allow for rapid ascent in the young may, paradoxically, interfere with adult creative achievement. At that later point, it is necessary for the aspiring creator to go against the crowd, rather than to deliver just what an audience wants in a way in which that audience can most readily apprehend and appreciate it.

Mozart's struggle against his father symbolized the ultimate costs of prodigiousness. Leopold had dominated his early life and, like many children, the young Wolfgang accepted—and perhaps craved—his father's approval, which had inspired his singular achievement. But Leopold was at base a conventional person with conventional ideas: he wanted Wolfgang to compose music that was acceptable to the courts (the "field" of the day), and he wanted Mozart to land a job as a Kapellmeister in one of the major courts of the day—not least so that the senior Mozarts would be well taken care of in their old age.

The young Mozart had no objection to fame, fortune, and personal and family security. But it gradually became clear that such attainments could be reached only at a high price: he had to kowtow to those in authority and he had to craft music to their liking.

Mozart's compositional genius had taken on a dynamic of its own. If by age fifteen (or even earlier) he already had mastered the compositional options of the time, he was faced with a stark choice: either continue, expert-style, to repeat himself or venture in new, relatively unexplored directions.

To move toward the unknown, Mozart had to make sharp and difficult breaks—a break from his teachers and models, a break from the accepted practices, and, most painfully, a break from his father. Perhaps the homage to Haydn, as the crowning act of his composition of string quartets, offered a means of easing this painful process—for he was simultaneously breaking new ground and yet confirming his tie to a tradition he prized.

The challenge Mozart confronted is one that every prodigy must face. The prodigy is marked by a fluent, perhaps even facile, mastery of an already existing domain. As we've noted, the prodigy in chess, music, or mathematics proceeds smoothly over ground that has already been covered by others in the culture. Moreover, the prodigy is rewarded for this fluency, inasmuch as most adults like nothing better than to behold a diminutive figure already accomplishing feats better than they could. The prodigy's domain has been chosen for him—by fate or family—and, at least during childhood, he need only revel in this fact.

Tiny figures grow to adult proportions, however, and novelty wanes. Indeed, the grown prodigy is indistinguishable from peers who were never prodigies but who, through dint of effort and training, are able to perform like accomplished adults in their chosen domain. More so than others, the prodigies have been rewarded precisely for being like those who are older and more established; but now the rewards cease.

Prodigies may suffer three fates. Some cannot recover from the loss of specialness, and suspend performance altogether, either temporarily or permanently. A psychologist who was once a musical prodigy, Jeanne Bamberger calls this condition the mid-life crisis of the musical performer. It tends to occur during the teen years. Subsequent to this crisis, the prodigy may return to the craft with renewed energy and increased understanding but, less happily, may instead move to totally different pursuits, including ones for which he or she has little talent. Such ex-prodigies want to realize their own ambitions rather than hone further the gifts that others have promoted.

Many prodigies simply continue to perform at a high level in their domain—they become bona fide adult experts. Former prodigies populate symphony orchestras, high school and college mathematics departments, and chess clubs. Part of this pattern is simply statistical: not every prodigy can become a star. But this pattern also reflects personality, for the motivations that spur prodigies differ from those that drive creators.

The rarest outcome is for the prodigy to evolve into a creator of the highest order. Such a transformation requires the will to change from one who follows to one who stands alone, and the skill and luck to effect that change. Picasso succeeded in doing so in painting, Auden in poetry. Among musicians, Mozart stands as the outstanding figure. Camille Saint-Saëns also successfully made the transition from prodigy to creator. Yet, struck by the limits of his creative output, his rival composer Hector Berlioz quipped that Saint-Saëns "knows everything, but he lacks inexperience" (quoted in Schonberg, 1969, p. 17).

For Mozart to become a creative Master, rather than a derivative expert, he had to turn his back on the models of his time and strike out on his own. By the age of twelve or so, he was already faced with the choice of creating increasingly iconoclastic works in familiar genres, or of deliberately restraining himself in order to satisfy the conventional tastes of his time.

Intellectually, Mozart had no ambivalence. He held nearly all his contemporaries in contempt and did not wish in any sense to emulate them. But personally and characterologically, the fascination with innovation was conflict-ridden, for Mozart was in part the amazing persona launched by his father and did not wish to countenance an explicit break. So, for well over a decade, Mozart engaged in a painful struggle with his father and all that he represented. On the surface the struggle covered many issues—where Mozart should live, where he should work, whom he should marry—but at the base, the struggle centered around control over Mozart's musical trajectory.

Kinds of Creative Mastery

As a creative Master, Mozart distinguished himself in two respects. The first is *producing permanent works in a genre*. Mozart contributed to the repertoire in over a dozen genres, ranging from concerti and symphonies to dances and serenades to operas, masses, oratorios, and requiems. (In this activity, Mozart resembles Picasso creating artworks and Virginia Woolf writing novels and essays.) Interestingly, Mozart's compositional output was not in itself record-breaking: Haydn composed 104 symphonies (compared to Mozart's 41), and such contemporaries as Antonio Salieri and Carl Ditters von Dittersdorf were able to compose "for the occasion" as speedily as Mozart. Mozart differed from contemporaries in the quality of his compositional output and not in the sheer number of works.

The second way Mozart distinguished himself as a Master was in *executing stylized performances*. When he performed or conducted publicly, he was not (typically) fashioning a new work; rather, he was interpreting a work that he (or another composer) had already fashioned. While there was room for limited experimentation and improvisation, the dimensions of the performance had been largely set before the artist stepped on stage. (In this activity, Mozart resembles Martha Graham performing a dance and Sarah Bernhardt facing an audience in a dramatic production.)

Supplementing these Mozartian pursuits, three additional realms of creativity should be identified. A third form of creation entails *solving recognized problems*. Here an individual working in a domain confronts a problem that is already known by contemporaries and succeeds in creating a solution to that problem. Scientists like James Watson and Francis Crick, who solved the structure of DNA; mathematicians like Andrew Wiles, who executed Fermat's last proof; and inventors like the Wright Brothers, who succeeded in devising a flying machine, are all creative problem solvers.

A fourth form of creation features *formulating a general framework or theory*. While individuals such as Freud, Darwin, Einstein, or Marx could be described as problem solvers, they are more aptly characterized as individuals who create new ways of thinking, new conceptualizations of phenomena. Often these new conceptualizations allow the solving of old problems, or the recognition of new ones, but the creative act inheres in the identification of elements, factors, and processes that can themselves incorporate problems and solutions.

A final form of creation returns us to the realm of performances, but this time *performances of high stake*. This is a situation where an individual's ability to perform creatively under stress could spell the difference between life and death, escape and injury. Telling illustrations of such creative activities are the strikes and fasts led by Mahatma Gandhi; neither Gandhi nor anyone else could anticipate the results of these acts of protest. Other instances include debates between presidential candidates, battles between opposing military groups, and—at a slightly less risky level—performances for career-making prizes in athletics or the arts.

Recognition of these varieties of creativity is important. First, we are reminded that there are several ways to be creative; one should not confuse one variety (say, problem solving or artistic production) with the others. Second, the life circumstances that lead individuals to one form of creativity may well differ from those that stimulate other forms. Scholars, who gain sustenance from the long years of research needed to solve a problem or create a theory, are quite different from performers, who feel most alive at the moment they face an audience. And there are even distinctions within these groups: problem solving is not of a piece with theory building, and stylized performances call on skills and psychic states quite different from those required for high-stakes performances.

So far as I can determine, Masters, Makers, Introspectors, and Influencers may be found within the ranks of each kind of creativity. But there may be affinities: for example, Makers may be attracted to the creation of new theories, and Influencers may favor high-stakes performances.

Mozart is unlikely to have made a sharp distinction between the various forms of creativity in which he was engaged. He lived, breathed, and loved music from the first days of consciousness—and he required little else for sustenance. The tranquillity many need to compose was unnecessary for Mozart; he could compose amid chaos. Nor did he require lengthy preparation time; he was able to compose even challenging pieces on demand (the string quartets being perhaps the most salient exception). Mozart heard music all the time in his head and was continually reconfiguring it; whether he was seated at the composition table, performing his own pieces, conducting or listening to those of others probably was not decisive. Indeed, we learn from anecdotes that Mozart listened aggressively to others' music; and, given the slightest opportunity or provocation, he did not hesitate to demonstrate how it could be improved. He knew his strengths and weaknesses: "I am no poet. I cannot distribute phrases with light and shadow; I am not a painter. I am a musician" (quoted in Turner, p. 200). He engaged in all musical creation, and happily so—his domain was Musical Creation, writ large.

Mozart in Later Life

To speak of Mozart in later life seems almost a contradiction in terms, since he died of a rheumatic ailment at the age of thirty-five. To the end of his life, Mozart kept composing at a steady rate; and it is commonly agreed that his last symphonies, operas, and religious music were distinguished by depth as well as serenity.

Yet, by ordinary standards, Mozart's last years were anything but happy or conducive to productivity. We might say that Mozart spent the first fifteen years of his life as a prodigy, the next ten becoming a world-class Master. But by the time Mozart reached the age of thirty, the happiest period of his life had ended—and he sensed as much. He had married, but quite possibly not to the woman he most craved. He had lost his mother and was shortly to lose his father. He was unable to achieve any lasting posts. He felt completely alienated from his native Salzburg, and increasingly unhappy in Vienna and other capitals. Even his most brilliant works, like *The Marriage of Figaro*, did not receive sufficient public acclaim. He lacked financial security and was reduced frequently to begging money from friends and acquaintances. And toward the end of his life, his health (and that of his wife) became precarious.

There is little question that Mozart was demoralized by this state of affairs. He was cognizant of the scope of his gifts; his unprecedented recognition in early life; the great hopes pinned on him by Leopold; and his own aspirations to achieve an influential post while remaining his own master. His letters record his depressions, his fluctuating moods, his embarrassments at having to pander to others. He noted sardonically that he was rewarded "too much for what I do, too little for what I could do" (quoted in Hildesheimer, 1982, p. 462). He wrote of "black thoughts" that he could banish only "with great effort" (quoted in Grove, p. 710).

Yet what is striking—and crucial for this inquiry—is that Mozart's output was largely unaffected by this downward turn in his fortunes. He composed two string quintets in 1787; his last three symphonies in 1788 (the triumphant Jupiter symphony during a time of poverty, pain, and pessimism); two quartets in 1789; his opera *Don Giovanni* premiered in 1787; *Cosi Fan Tutte* in 1790; *The Magic Flute* and *La Clemenza di Tito* in 1791, the last year of his life; and he composed dozens of other works as well. Indeed, before his final illness, he worked feverishly on a masonic cantata and on a requiem.

Clearly Mozart did not require a set of positive world experiences in order to compose. One could mount the reverse argument—that music constituted a compensatory activity for him—but then one might expect an ebb in productivity at a time when his personal situation was buoyed. The truth is, however, that there was hardly a fallow period in his entire life.

With Mozart, as with most extraordinary individuals, experiences are framed so that they undergird creative activity. Except for times when creators are actually incapacitated, the creative drive continues unabated, through emotional thick and thin.

Despite reversals, Mozart never lost faith in himself or his talent. He once declared, "I continue to compose because that fatigues me less than resting" (quoted in Hildesheimer, p. 193). Whether or not it is true that Mozart was busily composing music while his wife was giving birth in the next room, it is certainly true that Mozart could compose in a wide variety of circumstances and despite a broad range of personal moods. We might say that the creative composing muscle has a life of its own, and that it is very difficult to dislodge that muscle from its own rhythms of operation. As biographer W. J. Turner puts it:

> We have to try to realize with our utmost effort of the imagination how a mind like Mozart's never rested from music. Music was going on in his head continuously, probably even in his sleep, and his disinclination to teach was due to the fact that this disturbed his natural musical thinking in a way that dancing, playing billiards, bolt-shooting, and so on, did not. [pp. 263–64]

The World of Others

Mozart was certainly no hermit. Unlikely Beethoven, who could barely deal with other individuals, Mozart seems to have been affable enough. Throughout his life, he had friends—toward the end of his life, alas, ones who were quite dissolute. He did not refrain from rendering harsh judgments about others in his letters, but (perhaps following his father's rather fawning example) he was able nonetheless to maintain civil relationships with most persons.

As one of the greatest of operatic composers, Mozart was able to write music for a varied cast of characters, expressing an impressive range of messages and moods. He handled the complex interpersonal ties among different social classes in *The Marriage of Figaro;* the grandiose, flawed personality of *Don Giovanni;* and the shifting emotional configurations in *Cosi Fan Tutte* and *La Clemenza di Tito.*

Can we therefore conclude that Mozart was as outstanding in dealing with the world of persons as he was in mastering the symbolic domain of music? Might he qualify as an Introspector or even an Influencer?

I think not. Mozart introspected with great penetration about musical composition and performance in its technical aspects, but he showed little inclination to introspect about himself in person or in writing and proved remarkably inept at influencing others to do his bidding. Indeed, as his father came to realize, Wolfgang was constantly miscalculating his effects on others, and swinging unpredictably from excessive flattery to arbitrary confrontations. Perhaps, in truth, he was quite removed from other persons, caught up chiefly in his own world of sound patterns and the multifarious structures they yielded. As with other great creators, Mozart's relation to his work became all-important and all-determining.

Mozart stood out *not* in his understandings of specific human beings per se (even of himself), but rather in his capacity to preserve and capture human traits as part of the artistic task in which he was engaged with a librettist. Mozart knew the genres in which he was working, and he understood—from literature or from personal experience—the principal traits and motivations of the stock characters being portrayed. He went on to create musical language that fit perfectly with these characters as they underwent dramatic experiences. We might say, then, that as a superlatively talented craftsman, Mozart was able to introspect or to influence in the symbolic domain of music—but that these talents did not readily transfer to the mundane interchanges of life.

Mozart as Master

Among creators, there are two principal types: those who are constantly rejecting what they and others have done and who move almost compulsively in new directions; and those who early discover the soil they wish to toil, and do so with ever greater skill and finesse over the course of a life. Without question, Mozart belongs to the second group: while impatient with others and constantly challenging himself, he showed little inclination to create new genres, preferring instead to realize to perfection the genres of his time.

In part this tendency reflects the era in which he lived. In the seventeenth and eighteenth centuries, composers were craftsmen who worked in a well-recognized domain, creating works to order for their patrons. Certainly this is how Bach and Haydn—Mozart's greatest predecessors—thought of themselves, and what Leopold Mozart wished for his son. The tendency also reflects temperament. Though sympathetic to the political trends that were sweeping Europe, Mozart was hardly a revolutionary. He might well have been horrified by the French Revolution, even as Beethoven was stimulated by it.

Paradoxically, however, Mozart set the stage for musical revolution. He did so much in the way that Shakespeare, Goethe, and Keats did in their respective eras and genres—by so exhausting the existing lines of creation as to make it essentially impossible for those who succeeded them to follow in their footsteps. By being Mozart, he laid the groundwork for Beethoven and the Romantics, just as Brahms and Wagner stimulated the musical revolutions of Stravinsky and Schoenberg a century later.

Even among Masters, Mozart stands out. First of all, the evenness of his productivity and its steadily high quality were stunning. It is almost if, independent of the events in his personal life and in the wider society, Mozart's brain had been set to produce a certain number of melodies and compositions per unit of time. And as is well known, he was able to do so virtually without revision—conceiving works almost entirely in his head.

Second, Mozart represented an extreme in his amalgam of the young and foolish, on the one hand, and the mature and wise, on the other. All Masters (indeed, all creators) combine the childlike and the adultlike—indeed, many feel that this fusion constitutes an indispensable aspect of their genius. But in Mozart's case, his precocious musical development—coupled with his father's unrelenting promotion of Wolfgang's tender age—may have robbed him of the normal unfolding of developmental milestones; and so, in a sense, he felt licensed to maintain childlike behaviors and attitudes well beyond the usual limits.

The combination of child and adult attributes may have its rewards, however. Mozart's music retains a simplicity and elegance that we associate with the innocence of childhood. Sir Charles Stanford commented, "When you are a child, Mozart speaks to you as a child. No music could be more simple, more childlike. But when you are a man, you find to your astonishment that his music, which seemed childlike, is completely adult and mature" (quoted in Turner, p. 316).

Third, as noted, Mozart combined exquisite insights into human character in his music with a studied distance from (and surprisingly little understanding of) other people in ordinary life. Musical intelligence is significantly enriched by deep personal intelligences; Mozart possessed strands of personal intelligence, but either could not or did not choose to make use of these in his interactions with the rest of the world. This very distance from particular humans, however, may contribute to the universality of his music. Even more than that of other titans (and perhaps in a manner reminiscent of Bach), Mozart's work is free of the traces of individual personality.

Finally, Mozart has created our sense of the prodigy. There may have been prodigies before Mozart, and there have certainly been other prodigies since, but no person is likely to exemplify the child-as-adult as completely as did Mozart. Mozart is the standard against which other prodigies are judged, and this metric extends to other domains, including even that of psychology—the philosopher Stephen Toulmin (1978) dubbed the Russian polymath Lev Vygotsky "the Mozart of Psychology."

But Mozart not only represents the complete prodigy—he also reminds us that at least some prodigies can effect the transition from childlike feats to creations that help to define domains. Even two hundred years after his death, Mozart's compositions endure in popularity not only in the West but in every society to which they have been introduced. They are as universal as any form of art is likely to be. However, they represent the apothesosis of the classical genre—not the Making of a new domain. For an instance of that second extraordinary form of mind, we turn to another Austrian born exactly one century after Mozart: the psychologist Sigmund Freud.

FIVE

Maker:
The Case of Freud

"A Source of the Nile"

In 1896, Sigmund Freud was a forty-year-old neurologist-turned-psychologist living in obscurity in Vienna. Once a promising research scientist, he had turned away from the neurophysiological laboratory in order to understand (and aid) patients who displayed strange psychic symptoms. As Freud probed further into these disorders, he began to develop theories that his colleagues considered bizarre. Willingly or not, Freud was burning his bridges to the rest of the scientific and medical communities. Indeed, for a time, it appeared that the only other person who took Freud's ideas seriously was an equally aberrant physician named Wilhelm Fliess. Freud carried on a ten-year correspondence with Fliess, a convinced numerologist who believed that the major source of health problems was the nose.

As a result of his studies of disturbed patients (chiefly female hysterics) and his introspections about his own mind (including his dreams), Freud had come to a number of startling conclusions. He believed that there was an invisible stratum of mind—the unconscious—that constituted an indispensable component of mental life. He believed that "charged" experiences in early life, particularly if repressed, resulted in serious psychic pathology in later life. He believed that at the root of such disorders lay a sexual experience—typically, some kind of sexual abuse of the young child. And he believed that it was possible to uncover the content of the unconscious if one paid attention to such normal behaviors as jokes, slips of the tongue, free associations, and, above all, dreams. Convinced of the importance and originality of these discoveries, Freud spoke of a "solution to a more than thousand-year-old problem—a 'source of the Nile'" (quoted in Clark, 1980, p. 158); he quipped to Fliess that a marble tablet on his home would one day read: "Here, on July 24, 1895, the secret of the dream revealed itself to Dr. Sigm. Freud" (quoted in Masson, 1985, p. 417).

Freud sought forums in which to communicate his dramatic findings. In 1895 he drafted a dense tract that has come to be called "The Project for a Scientific Psychology," but he soon abandoned work on that virtually unreadable document. The next year he made a presentation to the Vienna Society of Psychiatry and Neurology, but found audience members skeptical or even dismissive. And finally he began work on what was to become his pathbreaking book, *The Interpretation of Dreams*, published in 1899.

Only with the publication of this major work did Freud finally hit his scholarly stride. Though the first edition of the book itself sold only a few hundred copies, Freud's ideas began to spread, first in Austria and then abroad. Publications about infantile sexuality, the operation of the unconscious, and the clinical practice of psychoanalysis poured forth to increasingly receptive audiences. Moreover, Freud's personal and intellectual charisma—as teacher, lecturer, propagandist for his ideas—stimulated the development of a cohort of followers who were to contribute to the promotion of his ideas. Within a decade, word of Freud's breathtaking insights had spread to the United

States; by the end of the First World War, Freud's ideas were widely known in medical and scholarly circles, and the Viennese thinker himself had achieved fame throughout the world.

The Early Years

While not particularly gifted in the typical domains of prodigiousness (indeed, he disliked music throughout his life), Freud could serve as the prototype of a scholastic prodigy. The product of a Jewish household, buoyed by proud parents and teachers, Freud was consistently at the top of his class in school. He read widely, as often as not in the original language of the publication. He was deeply versed in the arts, literature, philosophy, and science. His letters to friends reveal that he loved to analyze personal situations and to create dramatic enactments of human imbroglios. At various times, he considered the professions of medicine, law, and academic scholarship; indeed, if he had had his druthers, he would have elected to become a military commander, but Jews could not become officers in the Austro-Hungarian empire.

Freud knew that he was unusually talented in the intellectual realm; his early letters and journals suggest that the question at hand was not *whether* he would achieve significantly but rather in *which* professional or scholarly domain he would make his mark. While Freud's deepest passions ran to philosophical speculation, he realized that he was most likely to be able to have a comfortable existence if he pursued the career of a physician. So he studied medicine in Vienna and began a research career in the area of neurology. For a brief moment it appeared that Freud might achieve the fame he anticipated—and craved—from his discovery of the curative powers of cocaine. Freud's euphoria was short-lived, however; the effects of cocaine proved to be largely destructive. Moreover, to add to Freud's sense of deprivation, it was a close colleague, Carl Koller, who discovered the one unambiguously positive medical use of cocaine—as an anesthetic for eye surgery.

The most formative event in Freud's early career was his

postgraduate fellowship in Paris from October 1885 to February 1886. Freud attended the clinic run by Jean-Martin Charcot, a leading neuropsychiatrist of the era. At the Salpêtrière Hospital, Freud observed firsthand a fascinating range of neuroses, including several varieties of hysteria. Charcot presented cases in a dramatic fashion and brilliantly identified basic patterns that underlay the symptomatology. Freud never forgot Charcot's admonition that at the basis of hysteric disorders, one typically discovered "the sexual thing."

Freud was wandering at this point in his life—serving successively as an apprentice in several domains. To use the term of the psychoanalyst Erik Erikson, Freud's twenties had represented a "psychosocial moratorium." This period was punctuated by active experimentation with various life roles and styles, in an effort to discover which one fit best, which was most likely to lead to a productive identity for himself and a meaningful role in his community. Freud had considered the major professions and the major roles within medicine, without alighting on one that seemed right for him over the long haul.

Newly energized as a result of his contacts with Charcot, Freud returned to Vienna and began to work with an older colleague and acquaintance, Josef Breuer. Breuer described some of his impressions of hysteric patients and discussed at length the case of Fräulein Anna O. The two men developed a theory of the etiology of hysteria in emotionally charged events that had happened earlier in life—for example, an attempted seduction during the youth of the hysteric woman. Rather than consciously acknowledging these upsetting events, patients like Anna O. suppressed them, but at the cost of activating a physical symptom—such as hallucination, visual disturbances, or even paralysis. The privileged route to the alleviation of the symptomatology was a direct confrontation of the precipitating event—and that typically occurred as a result of what Anna O. herself called a "talking cure." As Breuer and Freud explained it:

[The cure] brings to an end the operative force of the idea which was not abreacted [worked through] in the first instance, by allowing its strangulated affect to find a way out through speech; and it subjects it to associative correction by introducing it into normal consciousness (under light hypnosis) or by removing it through the physician's suggestions. [quoted in Clark, 1980, p. 131]

The two physicians issued an important monograph, *Studies in Hysteria*, in 1895. But by that time their friendship was severely frayed. While willing to embrace a dynamic view of hysteria, Breuer became increasingly uncomfortable with discussion of unconscious processes, the transference of strong feelings between physician and patient, and the determining effects of sexual motives and motifs. In some ways he continued to admire Freud—he commented to Fliess that "Freud's intellect is at its highest. I gaze after him as a hen at a hawk" (quoted in Jones, 1961, p. 157); but he felt that he could not accompany him on these imaginative flights. And so, abandoned by his closest colleague and scorned by much of the Viennese medical establishment, Freud found himself pretty much alone at the time of his cutting-edge insights into the human mind.

The Makers' Patterns

There are striking regularities in the lives of Makers—those highly creative individuals who have invented or decisively altered domains. Based on these recurrent themes, I have created a prototypical Exemplary Maker (or E. M.) whose story I relate here. While not drawing explicit connections to all aspects of Freud's life, I will note some of the themes in his own biography.

E. M. is born in a community that is not at the very center of intellectual life, but close enough to allow contact with prevalent ideas and forces. As a young person, she is more likely to be seen as talented in a range of areas than as someone (like a Mozartian Master) who is targeted to pursue a specific domain or discipline. Her youth is colored with a bourgeois ethic of regular, disciplined work. Not excessively concerned about the area their daughter will ultimately pursue, parents (or guardians) make certain that E. M. works diligently and manifests progress over

time. Love and support may well be contingent upon achievement. Closer affective ties develop with relatives and family
friends who share interests with the young E. M.

Freud fits the bill here. He was born in Freiburg, Moravia, a
town of five thousand inhabitants situated 150 miles northeast
of Vienna. While his family moved to Vienna when Freud was
young, they remained remote from the intellectual, social, or
economic elites of the metropolis. His father was a ne'er-do-
well merchant who, as a Jew, was rejected from the reigning society. Freud's mother doted on him, as did a family nurse.
Because of Freud's scholastic gifts, he was given free rein in
choice of careers, but clearly his family expected him to become
a successful professional. Steps were taken to ensure that young
Sigmund had comfortable working surroundings; when he
complained about his sister's piano-playing, for example, the
family got rid of the instrument.

By the end of the second decade of life, E. M. takes off for a
center of cultural life. At the turn of the century, that typically
meant cities like Paris, London, or Vienna; today it is more
likely to be New York or Tokyo. There the individual makes a
tentative selection of a domain—not an entirely predictable selection, but always a choice from within a narrow band of options. (It was clear, for example, that Freud would become some
kind of professional or scholar.) She completes whatever training is needed in that field (without being overpowered by role
models). Sometimes the individual works directly with an impressive teacher or Master; sometimes the models are admired
paragons from history. More important, she sniffs out and
bands together with other young people who share her interests. They see themselves as young revolutionaries, who will
somehow make or remake their world.

We can recognize Freud here as well. In pursuing medical
studies in Vienna, he was moving to the center of his profession.
Freud was surrounded by a circle of friends who held him in
high regard; at first these friends were drawn from the ranks of
bright intellectuals, more generally; later they were more likely
to be fellow physicians. Freud gravitated toward older individuals who could guide him; in addition to his apprenticeship with

Charcot and his collaboration with Breuer, he spent critical years working in the institute of Ernest Brücke, a major scientist who guided Freud in neuroanatomical studies. As he moved toward psychiatric interests, Freud continued to search for colleagues; but with his ideas taking increasingly eccentric turns, only a scientific adventurer like Fliess was willing to join ranks with him. Once the psychoanalytic ideas had been formulated, Freud successfully linked with like-minded (if less impressive) contemporaries to launch a revolutionary movement.

E. M. must be ready to spend much time alone, exploring ideas and concepts that may make little sense to others initially. As the painter Françoise Gilot once put it, one should not consider becoming an artist unless one is prepared to spend seven hours a day in front of an empty canvas. At times the lack of contact with and comprehension by others can be so stressful that the individual risks having some kind of breakdown. Perhaps for that reason, nearly all creators crave some kind of close confidant at the times of their most important breakthroughs. These confidants provide intellectual support ("I understand what you are doing and I think it is sensible"), affective support ("I love you unreservedly"), or, optimally, both. Whether Picasso with Georges Braque, Martha Graham with Louis Horst, or Stravinsky with Serge Diaghilev, these individuals need an alter ego to keep them on course.

In the case of Freud, Breuer first provided the psychic support; when he could no longer bear this burden, Fliess appeared to fill the void. Fliess was willing to listen to Freud's wildest speculations without being judgmental (he expected similar indulgence from Freud), and he served as a kind of general confidant and supporter as well. Freud also received vital personal support from his large and caring family. While many Makers lose their parents at an early age, Freud's father survived until Freud was forty, and his doting mother until Freud was over seventy.

Typically, E. M. has grown dissatisfied with current work in a domain. Prevailing approaches block access to crucial phenomena or promising lines of inquiry. Sooner or later, she arrives at a new formulation that makes sense to her, that has the potential to affect others, and that may ultimately transform the domain in which she works. Try though she may, E. M. cannot control the uses to which others put her work; and she may well be disappointed or frustrated by these misuses, even as she is likely to be gratified (publicly or privately) by increasing signs of public recognition. Most Makers remain addicted to their work, however, and so they do not rest on their laurels. At approximately ten-year periods, they are able to produce further innovations, which repeat the initial cycle of loneliness, breakthrough, and attempts to garner support. These later innovations are typically more general and synthetic, often working through implications of the early work. However, there may also be dramatic shifts to new areas, either because the old area has been exhausted or because of the perception that greater glory or more intensive flow can be obtained by undertaking new challenges.

By the height of her career, E. M. has made a Faustian bargain. Work is all-important, and everything must be sacrificed for it. The endeavor is exciting, and others may well be drawn into it—but they do so at their peril. So long as they can help with the Maker's work, colleagues are likely to be cherished; but when their part in the play has been enacted, they are likely to be scuttled in favor of new collaborators and playmates. Creators rarely achieve perfection in the life and in the work (as Yeats lamented); rather, they must choose one of the options perceived by the ancient Romans: *libri* (books) or *liberi* (children). Of course, a person can strive to have both, but one option is likely to be shortchanged.

Freud's Pattern in Later Life

Freud again bears a reasonable resemblance to the prototypical pattern I have proposed. By the early years of this century, it had become clear to him—and those close to him—that he was no longer simply contributing to an already existing domain. Consequent upon his studies of hysteria and his probing examination of dreams, he had lain out a whole new terrain for exploration. That terrain included theoretical territory: frameworks that encompassed unconscious processes, early sexual development, human personality, and human motivation; it included clinical phenomena: the range of neurotic disorders, as well as vagaries in mundane human activities; and, increasingly, it included a technique for the investigation of the psyche: interpretation of dreams, free associations, the clinical methods of the newly minted domain of psychoanalysis.

As prodigious in his way as Mozart, Freud was the chief contributor to this burgeoning literature and ensemble of practices. He worked tirelessly—seeing patients throughout a long working day, relaxing in the evening with family and friends, then repairing to his study late at night to write until the wee hours. Some sense of his productivity can be gleaned from the fact that during a single two-month period in the middle of the First World War, the sixty-year-old Freud wrote six metapsychological papers. Without wishing to force Freud (or any other creator) into a rigid ten-year pattern, I point out that he presented his original clinical data and theoretical frameworks in the first years of the psychoanalytic movement; integrated these increasingly in the middle "metapsychological" phase; and then turned to wider social and political themes in the last years of his career.

More so than most scholars, Freud attempted to direct the uses to which his ideas were put. Long attracted by the military metaphor, Freud the Influencer saw himself as the leader of an embattled squadron of psychoanalytic workers—nearly all of whom he had selected himself. He created organizations that met regularly, debated ideas, issued journals and manifestos. He designated individuals as lieutenants—chief among them, the Swiss psychiatrist Carl Jung. He welcomed individuals into the fold, conferred honors upon them (including a special gold ring for elite members), and then abruptly banished them when their intellectual or personal loyalties came into question.

Life in the orbit of a great Maker is exciting but can be injurious to one's health. Like other Makers, Freud drew talented individuals toward him; but since Freud's loyalty was clearly to his work, rather than to them, he displayed little hesitation in distancing himself from those who could no longer contribute to his life's missions. Nearly all his original associates eventually broke with, or were cast aside by, Freud; in the end, his most faithful lieutenant proved to be his own daughter, Anna, who became the first child psychoanalyst.

Freud as a Creative Maker

A Master like Mozart has his domain virtually handed to him as part of his birthright; as a prodigy, his task is to become a superlative practitioner. The challenge to the prodigy-turned-expert is to transcend the achievement of fellow experts and acquire a distinctive form of mastery. Rarely does he question his domain, for he knows no other.

An individual who is not a prodigy in a recognized area faces a different set of opportunities and obstacles. She may wait until she encounters some kind of pursuit that engages her interest; this is what happened to the dancer Martha Graham, who had not even considered a career in dance until she began to attend dance performances while a teenager. She may choose an already existing domain and decide to compete with individuals who are already well launched in that area; this is what happened to Igor Stravinsky, who did not begin to study composition seriously until he had finished his law studies.

While Masters accept their domain, the Maker is typically not satisfied by a life working alongside others at the forefront of the domain. Rather, for reasons as varied as the individuals in question, the Maker moves regularly and repeatedly in new directions—confronting issues and challenges that are invisible to others or may even be actively resisted by them.

A schematic image may help here. Assume that the highly talented individual wants to make some kind of mark. Either one may head where others are already situated and best them at the competition—the advantage here is that the target is well known; the risk is that one might lose the competition. Or one may move where no one else is and attempt to create a new domain—the advantage here is that competition is virtually nonexistent; the disadvantage is that others may not appreciate the importance of what one is doing, and so one's discoveries and contributions may be ignored, either temporarily or permanently. Highly organized domains (like mathematics) tend to attract the centrists; less well articulated domains (like modern painting or evolutionary psychology) lure those who enjoy the periphery.

Freud's own gifts and limitations help us to understand the moves he made. By his own testimony, Freud was not impressive in the areas of logical-mathematical thinking or spatial reasoning. For example, he lamented: "I have an infamously low capability for visualizing spatial relationships which made the study of geometry and all subjects derived from it impossible to me" (quoted in Jones, p. 366). Yet these are precisely the areas that are important for the scientist.

On the other hand, Freud was extraordinarily gifted in language. Moreover, he had an abiding interest in the lives of other persons and in the workings of his own mind, and thus stood out in what I've termed the "personal intelligences." Moreover, his early skill in neuroanatomy and his subsequent immersion in the symptomatology of different groups of patients suggest special talent in "naturalist intelligence": the ability to recognize patterns in living phenomena. It made sense for Freud, who continued to think of himself as a scientist, to leverage his areas of strength, to forge a distinctive domain: one that drew on his linguistic, personal, and natural intelligences, while not calling in any strong sense on logical-mathematical or spatial intelligences.

What of the actual operation of Freud's mind as a Maker?

I see Freud as energized by three motivations: pleasure in classifying, lust for problem solving, passion for system building. In the manner of a good naturalist, Freud loved to take in as much data as he could and then try to organize them systematically. Initially, following Charcot, he performed such classifications over and over again with the neuroses; later in life, he applied a similar organizing scheme to the full range of the human personality configurations.

Second, Freud loved to identify puzzles and then solve them.

Whether in his personal life or his professional work, nothing pleased him more than to identify some kind of paradox and to ponder it. As a youth, he applied Talmudic reasoning to questions like the rationale for suicide and the place of women in the modern world; as the first psychoanalyst, he puzzled about whether sexual abuse had to happen in the flesh or only to be imagined and whether women exhibit a psychosexual quandary that mirrored the little boy's Oedipal complex.

After Freud had classified phenomena and puzzled out solutions, he wanted to synthesize the results of his work: this is where he became a system builder—one who creates a new theory and a new mode of treatment. Freud's legacy lies significantly in the complex system of explanation that he developed.

More so than many other investigators, Freud craved communication of his findings to a broader public. He was a brilliant communicator both orally and in writing; the success of psychoanalysis is as much a tribute to his communicating genius as to the power (or the validity) of the ideas. It is instructive that initially Freud tried to express his new ideas in a highly technical and scientific form; we see this working out of a special "new symbol system" in the turgid prose and difficult-to-decipher diagrams of the *Project* and *The Interpretation of Dreams*. Eventually, Freud came to realize that his ideas could equally well—and far more convincingly—be conveyed in everyday, nontechnical language. Both his oral (often impromptu) and written lectures are models of explanatory clarity.

The Domain and the Field

The prodigy and the Master have clear pursuits and audiences. Mozart wrote pieces in established genres for the nobility of Europe; their reactions to his music determined its success and its short-term survival value. If the fields of the time were not welcoming, Mozart's only recourse was to hope that a reconstituted field in the future might better appreciate the extent of his achievement.

With respect to a Maker like Freud, the situation is entirely different. By the time he put forth his most original ideas, Freud had already been completely marginalized in the domains that he had originally inhabited. Unless he was willing to wallow forever in obscurity, it became clear to Freud that he would have to create his own domain(s) and his own field(s).

Though it probably did not occur as directly as this suggests, Freud's mission after 1900 became clear. He had to identify individuals who were sympathetic to his work; support them in their own explorations; enable them to practice the clinical methods that he had invented; and create institutions and publications that would bring this new line of work to the fore and confer legitimacy upon it. The appeal of the ideas, the power of Freud's personality, and the timing of the contribution worked together in this instance—and within a quarter of a century, the domains and fields of psychoanalysis were an established fact throughout much of the Western world.

Phrasing it this way places the emphasis on the individual, perhaps unduly so. Makers cannot succeed unless there exists a domain that is waiting to be altered—in this case, the domains of psychiatry and psychology had clear gaps that Freud helped to address. (Evidence for this assertion comes from the fact that Pierre Janet, a French psychologist, was developing similar ideas at the time.) By the same token, since Freud had no power to compel assent to his theories, there had to be a set of individuals who were longing for the intellectual and personal leadership that he could supply. Initially, indeed, the members of his Wednesday evening fellowship constituted a motley crew of mavericks and second-raters; it is a tribute to Freud that he eventually attracted a far more impressive group of adherents within neighboring domains as well as in more remote fields, ranging from political science to literary criticism.

By my definition, a Maker is an individual who creates new domains or radically recasts an existing domain. Freud needs no defense on either score. And yet many individuals today question the significance of Freud's contribution. They point out that many of his assertions are by nature unprovable (as they cannot be disconfirmed, so they cannot be confirmed either) and argue, further, that those elements of the Freudian enterprise that have been subjected to empirical testing have not received much support.

I would readily concede that Freud is not a scientist, in the sense that one can carry out a systematic program of research on his ideas, a program that readily separates fact from fancy. But to judge Freud by this textbook view of science is to miss the point of his achievement.

A quintessential naturalist, Freud called attention to a whole range of human phenomena and processes that had at most been dimly sensed by other scholars, artists, and observers of human life. He put forth a first-draft (and sometimes a second-draft) way of thinking about these phenomena; he developed a number of promising conceptual tools and clinical techniques for securing more knowledge. While Freud solved certain problems, and enjoyed the process of problem solving, he is much more important as a problem *finder*—one who raises new questions—and a system builder—one who constructs a whole new framework, in this case for thinking about human behavior, motivation, and personality. So significant is this achievement that it is not easy to think about the human mind and personality in a pre-Freudian way; even critics often use the tools of psychodynamic thinking (without always being aware that they are doing so).

Even a book like this constitutes a tribute to Freud's discoveries. My discussions of early childhood take Freud's views as a point of departure. The emphasis on the significance of early biographical events owes much to Freud's way of thinking. It has become natural to interpret Mozart's personal zigzagging in terms of his relationship to his father, and to see Virginia Woolf's psyche—and sexual ambiguities—as a reflection of her relationship to parents and siblings. Freud's vivid depiction of the appeals and perils of the creative life also undergirds many contemporary analyses of these phenomena, including my own.

To dismiss Freud as a contributor to science is as erroneous as claiming that he has been "proved" correct. Much empirical evidence confirms the general outline of phenomena to which Freud first called attention: for example, the important, often determining, effects of early experience, ranging from sibling rivalries to various forms of identification with models; the role of unconscious (subliminal) processes in affecting behavior; and, recently, the claim that repression is a genuine psychological and neurological phenomenon. And while the specifics of his clinical techniques are no longer taken as gospel, the recognition that psychological problems are genuine and that they require treatment rather than embarrassment or denial, constitutes again a tribute to Freud's courage and his insights. It would be foolish to dismiss Marx just because his dream of communism has not survived—his economic analyses have proved far more enduring. It is equally foolish to dismiss Freud just because new forms of treatment have arisen—his view of the psyche continues to instruct.

Three Lessons: An Introduction

More so than Mozart (whose genius remains *sui generis*), Freud serves as an excellent introduction to three lessons that ordinary individuals can draw from the life experiences of an extraordinary individual. To begin with, from his childhood, Freud always devoted a considerable amount of time to reflection on his own experiences and his life options. And, indeed, as the founder of the psychoanalytic technique, he brought to a heightened plane the practice of introspection about one's experiences and one's dreams—with the aid of a sympathetic sounding board.

Second, Freud had a keen sense of his areas of strength and weakness. While lamenting his weaknesses, he did not dwell upon them. Instead, he turned his energies to activities where he had a clear-cut competitive advantage over others: the study of the mind in dysfunction; clinical investigation of psychopathology; the penning of convincing tracts; and the launching of an intellectual movement.

We all put a spin on experiences, seeing them as models, cautionary tales, precedents to be avoided at all costs, or setbacks from which we can learn and on which we can build. Freud provides a textbook example of an individual who was not undone by setbacks. The early years of his career were filled with defeats that would have stymied a less self-confident individual. While personally disappointed at his failure to make breakthrough discoveries in science, and hardly a Pollyanna in any sense, Freud never deviated from a belief in his abilities and in his potential to make important contributions. He took rejection not as a sign to give up but rather as a spur to recommit his energies—to weave together the various strands of his emerging understanding into a powerfully integrated approach to the human mind. In letters to Fliess at the time of his greatest discoveries, he confessed:

> If both of us are still granted a few more years for quiet work, we shall certainly leave behind something that can justify our experience. . . . No one even suspects that the dream is not nonsense but wish fulfillment. . . . I am pretty much alone here in the elucidation of the neuroses. They look upon me as pretty much of a monomanic, while I have the distinct feeling that I have touched upon one of the great secrets of nature. [quoted in Masson, p. 180]

Creators are masterful Framers of experience. Stravinsky was able to overlook the total rejection of his cantata *The King of the Stars* and the furious reaction to his revolutionary work *The Rite of Spring;* Picasso was so taken aback by early reactions to his iconclastic *Les desmoiselles d'Avignon* that he kept it hidden for years—but advanced to Cubism nonetheless. And so too, Freud could take rejections—not happily, perhaps, not without pain—and see in them the clues to future success. And when an opposite, more skeptical framing was needed, Freud could provide it as well. There is an amusing story of the time Carl Jung traveled to America and toured the East Coast, singing the praises of psychoanalysis. He wired cheerfully to his Master: "Psychoanalysis tremendous success in America." Freud wired back immediately: "What did you leave out?"

What enables a handful of persons to make creative contributions, while others of equal skill and commitment do not? The notion of *fruitful asynchrony* proves illuminating.

When studying prodigies, scholars have noticed the process of coincidence—the happy co-occurring of many factors, culminating in a child who is off the charts in at least one domain. In studying Makers, I have been struck by the importance of a contrasting factor. By invoking fruitful asynchrony, I seek to capture the ways creative individuals can turn to advantage their discrepancy from others in their time and in their domain.

Freud was in many ways an "outlier"—a Jew living in the midst of a gentile and largely anti-Semitic society; the youngest son of a father who was twice as old as his mother; a benchtop scientist whose chief skills and talents were not particularly relevant to his chosen career. And when he began to push forward his own developing ideas about the mind, he marginalized himself even further—losing the support of even his closest associate, Josef Breuer.

Thus Freud was certainly asynchronous in many ways from his surround. There was a marked chance that this marginality would result in a disjunction from the rest of society—either temporary or permanent. (In fact, in the mid-1890s, Freud may have suffered a breakdown.) However, Freud did not allow asynchronies to defeat him—instead, he exploited them. He learned much from his study of Judaism and his membership in an embattled tribe; he pondered the peculiarities of his own family relationships and discerned in them seeds of more universal personal relations; he abandoned those regions of science where he could not distinguish himself in favor of devising a domain in which his own strengths—perhaps uniquely—could be foregrounded. And when he began to have impact, he pushed his advantages as far as he could, even to the extent of injuring those who had once been closest to him.

One cannot choose the degree of marginality—that is given chiefly by circumstances. But one can choose the stance one adopts toward asynchrony. Framers of experience make a positive ally out of their asynchronies and thereby advance where others might fall by the wayside.

Of the various roles that we have described, Freud fits most comfortably into the category of Maker. But it would be unfair to Freud—and misleading for our study—were I to suggest that

Freud occupied only this creative role. His own writings show him to be a Master of the German language—indeed, he was awarded the prestigious Goethe Prize in 1930. The tremendous impact that psychoanalysis had in his time—and continues to have in ours—could not have come about had Freud not been an excellent Influencer. Freud influenced others directly through his spoken word, indirectly through the institutions he created and through his powerful writings.

And, finally, Freud peered deeply into his own psyche and into that of all human beings—he was one of the signal Introspectors of his time. It is fitting that Freud's works were published in England by another formidable Introspector, Virginia Woolf—and that she was one of the intelligentsia who welcomed Freud to England after he had escaped the Nazis at the end of his life.

SIX

Introspector: The Case of Woolf

Four Venues for Introspection

In the mid-1920s, when the British writer Virginia Woolf was in her early forties, she broke new ground in her literary production and beheld unfamiliar vistas in her personal life. She had published a tour de force, *Mrs. Dalloway*, a novel that portrayed a day in the life of a London hostess, and was beginning two self-consciously experimental novels, *To the Lighthouse* and *The Waves*. Continuing her incisive social criticism, she was preparing *A Room of One's Own*, a set of bold lectures on the conditions of woman as writer. For the first (and probably only) time, she embarked on a romance with another woman, the tempestuous and openly lesbian writer Vita Sackville-West. And despite continuing bouts of depression and episodes of mania, she led an extremely active social life, traveling through England and abroad with her husband, Leonard, and interacting on an almost daily basis with the public figures of her own circle of Bloomsbury and the larger London intelligentsia.

Woolf wrote of the public sphere, but her deeper interest lay in the nature of experience—her own experiences as Virginia Stephen Woolf, the experiences of those to whom she was close, the experiences of women (and, at times, of men) in her world. She was interested in the contents of those experiences—what it was like to be Virginia Woolf or a struggling woman writer named Mary Carmichael; but she was equally interested in the form and feeling of experience—what it is like to be conscious, to be joyful, to be mad. And increasingly, she sought to capture the rhythm and flow of experience in her fictional productions—earning her a prominent place, along with James Joyce and Marcel Proust, as one of the literary innovators of the era.

Among our creators, Virginia Woolf stands out as an Introspector—one who peered inward, seeking to understand herself as an individual, a woman, a human being. Of course, many individuals devote themselves to Introspection, but only a few can convincingly convey to others the core processes and insights of their introspections. We've seen that Sigmund Freud was also a master Introspector—indeed, a person who invented a method that allowed others to introspect. But Freud presented the fruits of his introspection in writings that are clinical in tone; and introspection serves as a *means* toward understanding human psychology in a scientific manner. To the extent that Mozart peered inward, such introspection left little trace in his letters or in those of his quoted statements that are not in dispute; excepting his epic struggle with his father, we need to infer aspects of his inner life primarily from his musical creations.

When I first began to study Virginia Woolf, I anticipated that the key to her introspections lay in the five large volumes of her diary, which she kept, often making daily entries, from 1915 until her death in 1941. And to be sure, these diaries prove an invaluable guide to Woolf's thoughts and activities over a quarter-century. Consider, for example, this personal account of an attack of madness:

No more of this. I reason. I take a census of happy people and unhappy. I brace myself to shove, to throw, to batter down. I begin to march blindly forward. I feel obstacles go down. I say it doesn't matter. Nothing matters. I become rigid and straight, & sleep again, & half wake & feel the wave beginning & watch the light whitening & wonder how, this time, breakfast & daylight will overcome it. [quoted in Bell, 1980, p. 110]

But three other sources prove equally revealing. Woolf was an inveterate letter writer, and her letters are among the most intimate documents about her life. Here she writes to her friend, author Gerald Brenan, about reactions to her work as a writer:

> Perhaps it is this lack of criticism, or rather the fact that I affect different people so differently, that makes it so difficult for me to write a good book. I always feel that nobody, except perhaps [famed novelist E. M.] Morgan Foster, lays hold of the thing I have done; they meet in conflict up in the air; and so I have to create the whole thing afresh for myself each time. Probably all writers now are in the same boat. It is the penalty we pay for breaking with tradition, and the solitude makes the writing more exciting though the being read less so. One ought to sink to the bottom of the sea, probably, and live along with one's words. But this is not quite sincere, for it is a great stimulus to be discussed and praised and blamed. [quoted in Banks, 1989, p. 195]

Woolf may have been the first woman to have achieved significant readership as an essayist in English—underscoring the difficulties confronted by women who wished to speak or write publicly from their own perspective. Here, in *A Room of One's Own*, she describes the obstacles faced in the past by any woman who would write:

> But for women, I thought, looking at the empty shelves, these difficulties were infinitely more formidable. In the first place, to have a room of her own, let alone a quiet room or a soundproof room, was out of the question . . . the indiffer-

ence of the world which Keats and Flaubert and other men of genius have found so hard to bear was in her case not indifference but hostility. The world did not say to her as it said to them, Write if you choose; it makes no difference to me. The world said with a guffaw, Write? What's the good of your writing? [Woolf, 1929, p. 52]

And in her novels, such as *To the Lighthouse*, Woolf pondered the nature and flow of human experience:

What is the meaning of life? That was all—a simple question; one that tended to close in on one with years. The great revelation had never come. Instead there were little daily miracles, illuminations, matches struck unexpectedly in the dark; here was one. This, that, and the other; herself and Charles Tansley and the breaking wave; Mrs. Ramsay bringing them together; Mrs. Ramsay saying, "Life stand still here." . . . In the midst of chaos there was shape; this eternal passing and flowing (she looked at the clouds going and the leaves shaking) was struck into stability. [Woolf, 1927, pp. 240–41]

There is no single, privileged window peering into Woolf's introspective mind. Woolf reflected in different ways for different purposes, and she captured those innermost thoughts across her diverse writings. Only through a blending of insights and impressions from diaries, letters, essays, and fictions can one penetrate to the essence—or, more properly, the essences—of Virginia Woolf.

A Remarkable Background

The product of a most unusual family, Virginia Stephen's early years were marked by many powerful and affecting experiences. Her mother, Julia Jackson, a beautiful and generous woman, gave birth to seven children and died when Virginia was only thirteen. Her father, Leslie Stephen, was a noted writer and critic and the founding editor of the ambitious *Dictionary of National Biography*. Publicly an attractive figure, he was stiff and ungiving at home.

Virginia grew up in a highly intellectual house, close to her older sister, Vanessa, and her two full brothers, Thoby and Adrian. Consistent with Victorian "protection" of women, Virginia and Vanessa received no formal education, while their brothers went off to Cambridge; but Virginia's parents did encourage their bright and energetic daughter to read and to write. Her youth was replete with the asynchronies of illness, death, and madness. By the age of twenty-two, she had lost both her parents and her half-sister, Stella; and twice during adolescence, Virginia had become mentally unbalanced.

Virginia Stephen's career began in earnest in the first years of the century, when she began to write book reviews for *The Times Literary Supplement*, *The Guardian*, *The Nation*, and other publications. Woolf read and wrote rapidly and proved able to penetrate, in remarkably few words, into the spirit of writers and their works. This apprenticeship of reviewing on deadline for pay contributed to her self-confidence, and within a decade she had begun to write novels. Her literary works of this period—*The Voyage Out* (1915) and *Night and Day* (1919) among them—were well received, and confirmed that Woolf was equally a Master of fiction.

Woolf's literary development coincided with her involvement in a remarkable group of young British intellectuals that soon came to be known as Bloomsbury. In its early years, the group included such future luminaries as the painter Duncan Grant, the art critics Clive Bell and Roger Fry, the author E. M. (Edward Morgan) Forster, the economist J. M. (John Maynard) Keynes, and the literary critics Desmond McCarthy and Lytton Strachey. No individuals were more important to the group than Virginia Stephen, her sister Vanessa (who married Clive Bell), their brother Thoby (until his untimely death from typhoid fever), and Virginia's soon-to-be husband, the journalist Leonard Woolf.

At first, Virginia conformed to the expectation that, as a woman, she would listen admiringly to the eloquent Cambridge-educated young men. But the mores of this iconoclastic group postulated that women had minds of their own, and they were expected to participate without inhibition in the intellectual give-and-take of the salon. Though somewhat diffident, Virginia showed herself equal to the men on this intellectual plane—and in all likelihood superior in her ability to enter into the worlds of other human beings.

There is little question that Virginia Woolf's later education took place in the exchanges among the members of the Bloomsbury group. What the men had attained from attending college, what Mozart attained from traveling through Europe and studying other composers, Virginia and Vanessa Stephen gleaned from their active membership over three decades in one of the more impressive groups of artists and intellectuals that ever assembled. From our vantage point, it appears that Virginia may have been the pivotal member of the Bloomsbury group—and perhaps its most brilliant as well.

A Focus on One's Own Experiences

Woolf had devoted her twenties to the mastery of expository writing, and her thirties to the mastery of the novel. Particularly because these attainments in themselves were remarkable for a woman without formal education, it would have been easy for her to rest on her laurels.

But, like other epoch-making creators, Woolf was impelled to reach further. The ambition she had observed in her father and then in the Bloomsbury circle had infused her own blood, and she was determined to make her mark as an artist. That mark, she suspected, lay in her capacity to capture and convey unique personal experiences.

Woolf did not need instructions about her marginality. She came from a background that was comfortably middle-class, yet she lived in a circle that was more attuned to the aristocracy. She was a woman in a world that was dominated by strong and ambitious males. In comparison to those who had attained acclaim in the world of arts and letters, she was peculiarly uneducated. Not without considerable ambivalence, she had married a man who came from a religious Jewish background.

Moreover, in addition to these demographic anomalies, Virginia Woolf deviated from others in two more profound ways. She was clearly sexually anomalous—among the terms that have been used to describe her are *androgynous, bisexual, neuter.* Perhaps owing to sexual attacks during her youth by both of her half-brothers, Woolf was not attracted physically to males and found the sexual act off-putting. As previously mentioned, at least once in her life she was strongly attracted to a woman—the writer Vita Sackville-West—but this physical relationship was rarely if ever consummated. She never considered herself a lesbian (a "sapphist")—rather, she saw herself as an artist having equally strong identifications with men and women.

Virginia Woolf was also, to use her own term, mad. Several times during her adolesent and adult life, she underwent periods of clinical depression, when she had to be isolated, kept under surveillance, and compelled to rest. More frequently, she oscillated between moods of mania and bouts of depression. These periods of illness often coincided with traumas in her own life—the death of a parent, the completion of a book—but there seems little question that they reflected a strain of manic-depressive disease in her family. In the end, unable to deal any longer with imaginary voices, severe psychic pain, and a sense of failure, Virginia Woolf committed suicide by drowning herself in a river that ran through her own property.

It was not easy for Virginia to speak about her sexual and psychotic experiences openly. This is hardly surprising, inasmuch as they are deeply personal, quite likely to be embarrassing, and prone to be misunderstood by others. Moreover, though the Bloomsbury group was shockingly explicit in comparison to contemporaries, even its members touched lightly on sensitive subjects and tended toward clever repartee rather than brutal candor.

Yet, preoccupied with her inner life, Virginia Woolf was determined to share her perspective with others. She sought to exploit her areas of strength: her knowledge of self and her skill at writing. A variety of literary and conversational modes were available and she made judicious use of each. Her novel *Orlando*, in which a man is transformed into a woman, offered her ample opportunity to explore the nature of sexuality; but she explored sexuality as well as her diaries, letters, and increasingly eloquent and pointed essays on women, writing, and "a room of one's own." Several of her novels, among them *The Voyage Out*, *Mrs. Dalloway*, and *The Waves*, attempted to convey madness, and she often, if delicately, described her moods and states in her diaries and letters.

Virginia Woolf saw men as self-confident egos putting forth strong theses on vital topics and defending them resolutely. In a lovely phrase, she pointed out their "formal railway line of sentence" (quoted in Banks, p. 188). Such phraseology did not reflect her world or her experience, however. Woolf regarded the individual not as a single dominant self, but rather as a collection of facets, a number of persons, who came to the fore at various times and struggled with one another. She sought to contrast the consciousnesses of different individuals as well as the different consciousnesses of the same individual.

Especially in her literary creations, Woolf avoided ponderous political, religious, or cultural themes. For Woolf, revelations of meaning occurred in those moments caught on the fly, where a spark flew, an insight clicked, a flittering glimpse or experience conveyed an important truth—"the sealing matter cracks, in floods reality" (Woolf, 1985, p. 142). The topics of her most daring books—a day in the life of a hostess, a trip to a lighthouse, six different perspectives on a friend who had died—are deliberately mundane, for Woolf felt that the trivial events of the day were likely to harbor profound insights. "What a phantasmagoria the mind is and meeting-place of dissemblables," declared one of her characters. "At one moment we deplore our birth and state and aspire to an ascetic exaltation. The next we are overcome by the smell of some old garden path and weep to hear the thrushes sing" (Woolf, 1928, p. 176).

Finally, and most ambitiously, Woolf wanted to convey the texture of quotidian experience. Given few models for this endeavor, Woolf was compelled to experiment with the sentence, the paragraph, the literary form. She wrote of a new stylistic device: "a sight, an emotion, creates this wave, long before it makes words to fit in; and in writing one has to recapture this and set this working (which has nothing apparently to do with words) and then, as it breaks and tumbles in the mind, it makes words to fit it" (quoted in Banks, p. 204). And she sought to convey one's feelings upon entering this new literary territory:

> I believe that the main thing in beginning a novel is to feel, not that you can write it, but that it exists on the far side of a gulf, which words can't cross; that it's to be pulled through only in a breathless anguish. Now when I sit down to write an article, I have a net of words which will come down on the idea certainly in an hour or so. But a novel, as I say, to be good, should seem, before one writes it, something unwriteable, but only visible. . . . I assure you, all my novels were first rate before they were written. [quoted in Banks, p. 238]

Woolf knew that she could never be completely successful in this endeavor—experiences are not words—and she questioned the existence of a privileged way of creeping up on experience and nabbing it. But others' (and her own) judgments of her own works are closely linked to an assessment of the degree to which she successfully apprehended the nature of conscious experience.

Among the Introspectors

In centuries past, philosophers like Plato, poets like Dante, diarists like Samuel Pepys, and essayists like Montaigne have probed the depths of their own spirits and of human experience more broadly. As we move to the twentieth century, there is hardly a literary figure or continental philosopher of significance who did not seek to convey something of his or her own experiences. In a broad sense, Woolf belongs to the same philosophical species as Kierkegaard, Nietzsche, Sartre, Frantz Fanon, and Simone Weil; the same literary species as Marcel Proust, James Joyce, and William Faulkner; the same as the occasional inward-directed behavioral scientist, like Sigmund Freud or Claude

Lévi-Strauss; and in the parade of essayists and diarists like Anaïs Nin, Witold Gombrowicz, and James Baldwin.

By and large, creative artists and scientists introspect in the West as a means of securing material for their works. Freud wanted to understand his mind as an example of all minds; Woolf sought to re-create her consciousness, and consciousness in general, in her writing. An entirely different tradition of introspection is associated with Eastern societies, such as those cultures influenced by Buddhism. Individuals involved in meditation, and other modes of spiritual attention, can bring introspection to an exquisite point of development and they may be able to help others achieve comparable mental states. But such introspective activity is carried out quite apart from any desire to make new objects; the activity is its own meaning, its own reward.

In contrast, if they are to be recognized by the field, Introspectors in Western societies must master a domain of communication—a public symbol system. Usually that will be the written word, though there are certainly introspective dancers, like Martha Graham, and painters, like Francis Bacon and Mark Rothko. Like the Influencer, the Introspector needs an understanding of other individuals. On occasion, as in the case of Virginia Woolf, he may also contribute to the creation of a new domain—in this instance, the Making of the experimental novel. But his primary challenge is to peer deeply into his own psyche, to understand himself in a way that others do not routinely understand themselves, as individuals, as members of a group, or as human beings.

What of the validity of introspections? After all, when it comes to knowledge of the physical or biological world, any trained individual can gain access to the same body of information; and when it comes to knowledge of other persons, these data are also open for inspection. But with respect to knowledge of oneself, clearly the knower has privileged information, data not available to others. It is conceivable that the aspiring Introspector will relate a compelling story that is not valid; or, conversely, that a factually accurate account will strike others as unconvincing.

These questions lurk as we consider Virginia Woolf. At any number of points, she conceded that her diary was not a particularly personal document, and wished that she could convert it into a "genuine" diary. She once exclaimed, "How it would interest me if this diary were ever to become a real diary: something in which I could see changes, trace moods developing . . . but then I should have to speak of the soul, and did I not banish the soul when I began? What happens is, as usual, that I'm going to write about the soul & life breaks in" (quoted in Bell, 1978, p. 234). Her husband, Leonard, once skipped over several pages of the diary after muttering that they had "not a word of truth in them" (quoted in Simons, 1990, p. 174). Virginia Woolf was a famous gossip, and many contemporaries felt that she much preferred a phantasm well told to a truthful rendition. Moreover, once she had attained a certain notoriety, it was evident that her letters and diaries would eventually be published; in some passages, one has the sense that she is performing for a future readership or rehearsing for a later work of fiction.

Were we restricted to only one source of introspective information about Woolf, I would hesitate to accept its evidence as reliable. Because Woolf wrote for so many years in several different genres, however, we can see whether the strands that emerge from one source (say, the diaries) are consistent with those that come through from the other literary documents—and, for that matter, from other lines of evidence from contemporary writings and figures. To put the matter a bit technically, the various lines of evidence can serve as controls for one another, and one can triangulate them in order to arrive at a fuller and, one expects, more veridical picture of the Introspector.

The penchant for introspecting is not difficult to detect (nor is its absence—say, in Mozart or, by his own testimony, in Keats). But the accuracy of the introspections can be assessed only by the weighing of such sources as are available—in terms of consistency with one another and coherence with our broader knowledge of human nature, including our knowledge of ourselves. After all, in some respects, we all partake of the same experiential flux.

Here an intriguing conundrum emerges. In Virginia Woolf's view, many individuals, especially men, seek a general synthetic account of themselves. Others, especially women, are suspicious of elegant and unimodal accounts; their experience suggests many fragmentary and somewhat contradictory components. Woolf declared to her diary, "How queer to have so many selves. How bewildering" (quoted in Bell, 1983, IV 39). A Woolf alter ego character named Rhoda complains recurrently that she has no face, and Woolf once lamented, after visiting Lady Ottoline Morrell, that she herself had no inner life. Her Orlando declares (somewhat outrageously), "If there are (at a venture) seventy-six different times all ticking in the mind at once, how many different people are there not—Heaven help us—all having lodgement at one time or another in the human spirit? Some say two thousand and fifty two" (Woolf, 1982, p. 308). Woolf provided ample evidence of this multiplicity from her internally tempestuous life and her scattershot writings. Accordingly, those biographers in search of a single "through line" will be more frustrated than those who revel in particularity and fragmentariness.

Although Virginia Woolf made reflections about "women" and "woman" central aspects of her work, in most particulars she remains an example of what could be termed a "masculine" view of creativity: the solitary Maker in his room, creating works that stretch or even remake a domain. Revealingly, most of Woolf's female protagonists were not creative artists or scientists: rather she wrote about women whose lives were chiefly domestic, women who distinguished themselves as wives, mothers, homemakers, or hostesses. Woolf respected these achievements, which were those of her beloved mother. She did not explicitly treat an intriguing possibility: that women have traditionally been creative precisely in those areas that are local, that impact chiefly on those within one's immediate circle, that can remain fertile only because one chooses not to have a "room of one's own" and to remain always "on call" for those dependent upon oneself. The entire history of such forms of "female generativity" remains to be written.

Creativity and Madness

It is relatively easy to relate to individuals in terms of their gender and their humanity; it is far more difficult to approach and to evaluate someone who is in some sense disturbed.

While revisionists have occasionally challenged the diagnosis, there was little question throughout Virginia Woolf's life that she was suffering from serious mental illness. To begin with, mental illness had been reported among members of her family on both sides, and her father suffered from depression. As early as adolescence, she had been incapacitated by breakdowns; these episodes recurred throughout her life; medical specialists concurred in the diagnosis. Woolf spoke and wrote readily about her desire to be sane, about her writing as a means of maintaining (and testing) her sanity, and about the experiences of being out of one's mind. She was preoccupied with suicide from an early age and attempted to take her own life while still a youth; in retrospect, she seemed destined to commit suicide, most probably by drowning.

Clearly, a touch of mental illness is no guarantor of creativity, but evidence has accumulated that a higher proportion of bipolar disease exists among the relatives of writers than is found in other populations. This finding is counterintuitive, since one would expect this disease to be equally prevalent among the families of other types of artists and creators.

We are far from understanding the reasons for this apparent correlation. The phenomenology is less mysterious, however. During manic phases, writers take in vast amounts of experience and, spurning rest, free-associate orally, darting across broad categories, in enormous bouts of productivity. In Quentin Bell's phrase, Virginia Woolf's imagination was equipped with an accelerator but no brakes (Bell, 1972, vol. 1, p. 148). As Leonard Woolf described it: "In the manic stage she was extremely excited; the mind raced; she talked volubly and, at the height of the attack, incoherently; she had delusions and heard voices, for instance she told me that in her second attack she heard the birds in the garden outside her window talking

Greek; she was violent with the nurses" (L. Woolf, 1964, pp. 76–77).

These fecund periods are important—indeed, precious—for writers. We get a sense of an alert though agitated mental state in passages like these:

> . . . and now all these people (for she returned to the Broad Walk) . . . the stone basins, the prim flowers, the old men and women, invalids, most of them in Bath chairs—all seemed, after Edinburgh, so queer. And Maisie Johnson, as she joined that gently trudging, vaguely gazing, breeze-kissed company—squirrels perching and preening, sparrow fountains fluttering for crumbs, dogs busy with the railings, busy with each other, while the soft warm air washed over them and lent to the fixed unsurprised gaze with which they received life something whimsical and mollified—Maisie Johnson positively felt she must cry Oh! [Woolf, 1925, p. 26]

During times of relative tranquillity, formerly manic writers can reflect on their experiences and cast a critical eye upon their drafts. The costs of this heightened excitement are reciprocal periods of depression, when one is unable to work, inclined to despise one's work, and perhaps driven toward suicide. Fortunately, this disease can now be largely controlled through medication, though possibly at the cost of a diminished zeal for writing.

Even in cases where a person has a strong biological proclivity for a disease, actual episodes may still be triggered by exogenous events. Virginia Woolf provides evidence for the environmental as well as the biological origins of mental illness. Painful episodes in early life—deaths of loved ones, sexual abuse by half-brothers—would certainly traumatize a sensitive young woman. Subtle messages of vulnerability on the part of grieving parents, and pressures to serve as a glue for a fragmented family, might also instigate bouts of illness. Virginia Woolf was ambivalent about the experience of completing a book, and terrified at the prospect of negative reviews; at such times she was particularly at risk for depression. And the objective factors of the last years of her life—the death of many friends, the rise of fascism (and anti-Semitism), bombs dropping on Britain, her own declining health—practically ensured future bouts of illness, if not the ultimate escape through suicide.

Each aspect of her marginality contributed to the specialness of Woolf's voice and her vision—in our terms, she was able to exploit her asynchronies in a fruitful way. I maintain, however, that extra leverage on the nature of conscious experience came from her immersion in the worlds of madness. Not only was she able in her writings to convey the fragmented nature of mania and the despair of depression, but the precariousness of her sanity made her especially sensitive to the miracles of conscious experience, her precious moments of lucidity, revelation, and epiphany.

Woolf as Artist

As an artist Virginia Woolf was extremely ambitious for herself and her work. From a relatively early point in her career, she saw herself as part of a talented elite. "I've never met a writer who did not nurse an enormous vanity," she wrote in 1913 (quoted in Banks, p. 79). She had confidence in her talent: "Give me no illness for a year, two years, and I could write three novels straight off" (p. 201). She compared herself to the major male authors of her own time—somewhat dismissive of Arnold Bennett and John Galsworthy, uncertain about Thomas Hardy, fraternal (if competitive) with E. M. Forster and T. S. Eliot, angered by James Joyce, and overwhelmed by Marcel Proust. With respect to women artists, she was unfailingly competitive—so much so that she could not appreciate their strengths, with the occasional exception of the short story writer Katherine Mansfield (who died young) and the novelist Vita Sackville-West (who became her lover).

Following her apprenticeship, Woolf came increasingly to feel that the writer had to be a perpetual experimenter. She had little respect for those writers who found and adhered to a formula; or for those who wrote only short occasional pieces. A writer, in her view, had to be at her desk all the time, continually creating new materials, continually pushing the envelope, especially in matters of form. She thought perpetually about literature: "I am ashamed, or perhaps proud, to say how much of my time is spent in thinking, thinking about literature. I doubt whether anything else in life is much worth having" (quoted in Banks, page 146). She once declared, "I have to some extent forced myself to break every mold and find a fresh form of being, that is of expression, for everything I feel and think. So that when it is working I get the sense of being fully energized—nothing stunted" (quoted in Simons, 1990, p. 188).

Living on the literary edge is the incubus of the Maker: as soon as one breakthrough is achieved, one must push on to the next. For some individuals, including Woolf at times, this "high-wire act"—not entirely remote from a high-stakes performance—can be very energizing. "I'm the hare, a long way ahead of the hounds, my critics," she crooned (quoted in Bell, 1983, p. 45). "What's the point of writing if one doesn't make a fool of himself?" she queried (quoted in Banks, p. 280). She knew how to frame experiences: "I'm fundamentally, I think, an outsider. I do my best work and feel most braced with my back to the wall" (quoted in Bell, 1984, p. 189). And yet, this pattern of existence is bound to be stressful, particularly when the effects of one's experimentation are directly measurable by the receptivity of the field: number of reviews, their positive or critical tone, and the sales of the book. More than happens with tough-skinned artists, Woolf's personal seismograph responded to every rave and to every pan.

But Woolf's books were far more than a vessel for her ambition and her competitiveness. They represented for her, as they do for any serious artist, the domain in which she worked out issues and feelings of concern. And with each literary achievement, she delved more deeply into her own psyche, including its most vulnerable crevices. In *To the Lighthouse* she dealt directly with her strong feelings toward her late mother and father; in *Orlando* she came to grips with her increasing sense of androgyny; her experiences of madness were probed at length in *Mrs. Dalloway*; and the loss of the best of the younger generation, and the nearness of death for the older, became her pre-occupation in *The Waves*.

Her writings also bear witness to Woolf's continuing efforts to capture the operation of consciousness, momentary experience, the mysterious moves of the mind. Probably more than anything else, Woolf came to believe that she had been put on earth as a writer in order to document what it was like to be a thinking, feeling, sensing human being. Other intellectuals might approach this issue through philosophy, psychology, or the portrayal of other persons in other times; on occasion, Woolf would attempt this feat through letters, diary entries, and essays. But she would do so in the most profound way through the creation of characters and scenes from her own time, sphere of society, and personal insight into the vagaries of human consciousness. She wanted above all to be judged by the extent to which this mission had succeeded. Though subjected to bouts of depression, she was able time and again to find new reasons to live: "I always remember the saying that at one's lowest ebb one is nearest a true vision" (quoted in Bell, 1977, p. 298). Only when the burden of living with madness became too heavy did she take her own life.

Woolf sought insight into the mind for its own sake; as an artist, she had few ulterior motives and few illusions about the likelihood that art could alter society. (Here, again, she ridiculed the grandiose male perspective on such matters.) In this respect, the Introspector differs most profoundly from the Influencer. The Influencer begins with knowledge of individuals—herself and others—but these are a means to an end: the desire in some way to alter the society (local or global) in which one lives. Perhaps at the start of his adult life (as it happened, residing in the London where Virginia Woolf was growing up), Mohandas Gandhi was preoccupied with his own mind; but by the time he had evolved into the Mahatma, it had become his fate to influence the world.

SEVEN

Influencer:
The Case of Gandhi

Productive and Destructive Protests

In 1918, Mahatma Gandhi, just shy of the age of fifty, intervened in a delicate labor dispute in the industrial city of Ahmedabad in West Central India. On one side of the dispute was
Ambalal Sarabhai, head of a distinguished Indian family. That
family, successful mill owners, had hosted Gandhi during his
residence at a local ashram. On the other side of the dispute
were the textile workers at the mills of the Sarabhai family.
During a time of large profits, high taxes, and marked inflation,
the mill workers felt inadequately compensated—they sought a
35 percent increase in salary.

Gandhi analyzed the situation carefully. After early attempts
at arbitration failed, he called on the workers to behave in an exemplary manner during a strike: no violence, no begging, no
molesting of strikebreakers; they must hold firm and find other

means of surviving during the strike. In turn Gandhi would push for an equitable increase in salary. When the strikers showed signs of becoming restive, Gandhi intervened again. This time he decided to fast—to put his own well-being on the line—until both sides had agreed upon a solution. As Gandhi put it:

> In my opinion I would have been untrue to my maker and to the cause I was espousing if I had acted otherwise. . . . I felt that it was a sacred moment for me, my faith was on the anvil, and I had no hesitation to rising and declaring to the men that a breach of their vow so solemnly taken was unendurable by me and that I would not take any food until they had the 35 per cent increase given or until they had falled. [quoted in Erikson, 1969, p. 51]

At first the mill owners were infuriated by the strike; they stood firm at their "best offer" of a 20 percent pay increase. Gandhi sought a solution where each party felt that its concerns had been honored. Ultimately he fashioned an agreement in which the millhands received their desired 35 percent one day (hence satisfying their own aims), 20 percent the next day (mollifying the mill owners), and then a perpetual increase of 27.5 percent, the arithmetical compromise. This compromise agreed upon, the strike ended. Perhaps more important, a lasting method of arbitration had been put in place. As biographer Judith Brown puts it:

> [Gandhi's] Ahmedabad campaign demonstrated not only the viability of satyagraha [nonviolent protest] in a further type of conflict but also many of the characteristics of his campaigns which were to recur wherever he had some real control—the search for a peaceful solution at the outset, the sacred pledge at the heart of the struggle, strict discipline and self-improvement among the participants, effective publicity, generation of an ambience of moral authority and pressure, and finally a compromise solution to save the face and honor of all concerned. [1989, p. 121]

A few years after the strike, in 1922, Gandhi identified another trouble spot that seemed ripe for intervention: the group of backward peasant villages in the small county of Bardoli near Bombay. Gandhi wanted to show the British government that it could not govern by intimidation and that it ought to grant India a greater degree of independence. He called for nonviolent resistance in this county.

But while Gandhi was leading a protest in Bardoli, violence exploded in a small town called Chauri Chaura, 800 miles away. During a legal process, an altercation broke out among members of an unruly crowd and the constables. When the constables ran out of ammunition, they withdrew to the city hall for safety. The crowd then set fire to the city hall, and when the constables escaped, twenty-one policemen and an inspector were hacked or burned to pieces by the raging mob. Hearing of this action, Gandhi became completely distraught. In his words, "No provocation can possibly justify brutal murder of men who had been rendered defenseless and who had virtually thrown himself on the mercy of the mob" (quoted in Fischer, 1983, p. 170). He reluctantly concluded that "there is not yet in India that truthful and nonviolent atmosphere which and which alone can justify mass disobedience" (p. 170).

Gandhi was so appalled by the event that he suspended the campaign in Bardoli and canceled all activities of protest throughout India. Hoping that all was not lost, he declared: "The movement had unconsciously drifted from the right path. We have come back to our mooring and we can again go straight ahead. If we learn the full lesson of this tragedy, we can turn a curse into a blessing" (Brown, 1989, p. 167). Nonetheless, Gandhi was arrested shortly thereafter on the charge of sedition. In a memorable trial, both he and the presiding judge acknowledged that they resembled actors performing in a drama scripted by more powerful forces. At the close, Judge Robert Broomfield sentenced Gandhi to six years in jail.

Makers and Influencers

In my earlier study of seven Makers, one individual did not fit the patterns as snugly as the others: Mahatma Gandhi. Makers generally direct their work toward individuals who already have some sophistication in the relevant domain: Freud was addressing other physicians and psychologists, Stravinsky was creating symphonic works and ballets for the committed musical public. But as a political and religious innovator, Gandhi was not preaching to the converted. It was his job to convince ordinary individuals from diverse backgrounds that his ideas about human nature, his recommendations about the optimal way to resolve conflicts, were superior to those to which they had previously adhered. To use a phrase from an earlier work of mine, this political leader had to find a way of addressing the unschooled mind.

The terms *Makers* and *Influencers* may draw from different realms of discourse, but these two populations of exemplary extraordinary minds have definite similarities.* Both sets of individuals are defined by the fact that they ultimately exert significant effects on the thoughts, feelings, or behaviors of others.

We cannot readily distinguish Makers from Influencers in terms of intent or degree of influence. A more promising route is to contrast the *directness* of their approaches. Influencers affect followers or the general public *directly* by virtue of the messages they convey and the policies they execute. Makers influence members of the domain and of the general public *indirectly*, by virtue of the particular symbolic products they create: written works, theories, bodies of science, organizational charts, works of art. In terms of our earlier developmental discussion, the Influencer operates person-to-person, the Maker or Master through the creation of a symbolic object or product, which in turn exerts influences upon others. Both Winston Churchill and Albert Einstein influenced the outcome of the Second World War: Churchill *directly* by his inspiration and guidance of the British population, Einstein *indirectly* by his theory that foreshadowed and facilitated the construction of the atomic bomb.

*From here on, I use the word *Influencer* to denote leaders, except in cases when I am referring directly to my earlier studies of leadership—just as I have used the word *Maker* to refer to highly creative individuals.

Most students of influence—most theorists of leadership—have focused on the power of the leader, the policies that he or she pursues, the relation of the leader to the public. Psychologists have directed their attention to the personality of leaders; following Freud's example, they have examined motivations, anxieties, battles the leaders have fought in their personal lives. I argue that our understanding of influence can be significantly enhanced if we take a *cognitive* view; according to this stance, influence occurs significantly in a set of exchanges between the minds of leaders and the minds of followers. The principal vehicle of influence is the story; an Influencer achieves effectiveness by embodying in his or her life the story that he or she relates.

In the academic discourse of today, stories and narratives have become very popular, and I need to indicate why I have chosen this terminology. As I see it, Influencers are trying to bring about changes in the ways their constituencies think and behave. To do this effectively, they need to mobilize the thought processes of their followers. A powerful means of achieving this effect is the creation of a narrative in which they make common bond with their followers; by describing goals they seek in common, obstacles that lie in the way, measures for dealing with these obstacles, milestones along the way, and promise that the desired utopia can eventually be achieved. Their dramatic "story" is most likely to be effective if they do not merely relate the story with effectiveness, but if in some sense their own lives capture the essence of that story and convey it convincingly to others.

Note that a story is not merely a "message" or a "vision." It is a full-fledged drama, one that grows naturally out of the life experiences of the Influencer, and one that seeks to envelop the audience in the same quest. One might say that such a narrative marshals "existential intelligence"—the capacity to address issues of being and meaning about which individuals care most profoundly. Individuals are prompted to change when they identify with an inspirational figure and an inspirational message; for human beings, compelling narratives are most likely to stimulate such identification.

Mahatma Gandhi illustrates these processes at work. Gandhi came of age at a time when the Indian subcontinent was completely subservient to the British Empire. It was natural to think of the British Empire as powerful and influential, colonial India as weak and without direction. As Indians became cognizant of the injustice of their situation, they grew impatient with British dominance—much as the upstart American colonists had almost two centuries ago. For most individuals, the increasing tension between the two sides was seen as leading inevitably to armed conflict, with considerable blood being shed on both sides.

Through a lengthy process of self-examination, study of history, and experiments that he himself had carried out in South Africa, Mahatma Gandhi became convinced of another way to resolve this dilemma. The conflict did not have to be conceived of as Powerful Britain versus Impotent India (or, for that matter, as Righteous India versus Evil England), any more than the struggle between millhands and mill owners had to be seen as Right versus Wrong. Gandhi called on human beings to imagine another, more hopeful scenario, one in which both parties engaged in a common search for a state of affairs in which each achieved legitimate status. Conflicts need not entail violence— they can proceed by a logic that makes both parties feel legitimate, even ennobled. This was a new, more inclusive story—one in which onetime rivals suppressed their differences in favor of a joint pursuit.

Gandhi did not just relate this visionary narrative. He embodied its drama in his own life, in his attitudes and his practices. He neither demonized Britain nor glorified India. Rather, he strove valiantly to discover the strengths, the fears, and the legitimate desires of both parties. And when it came to an actual conflict, Gandhi resolutely refused to arm himself—or his followers. Following the principles of *satyagraha* (nonviolent resistance), their approach to the conflict must be completely peaceful, nonviolent. It was better to die in the course of a peaceful resistance than to triumph by superior arms.

Of course, Gandhi recognized that situations were not always resolved so peacefully. Given the power of the unschooled mind, enemies were easy to demonize; and given the prevalence of weapons and the heat of passion, it was all too easy for peaceful resistance to yield to armed conflict. Gandhi showed that he was prepared to lead the cause of nonviolent resistance, even at the cost of his life.

The Influencers' Patterns

As with my studies of Makers and Masters, I probed the area of Influence through a series of case studies. Emma Laskin and I conducted detailed studies of eleven leaders, and added a survey of ten leaders of the Second World War. These studies led to the description of an ideal-type Influencer, whom I've dubbed E. I. (for Exemplary Influencer).

Exemplary Influencers arise from a wide gamut of circumstances. Franklin Roosevelt and Chiang Kai-shek led childhoods of material comfort, while George Marshall and Benito Mussolini came from families that were impoverished. Except for those (like the anthropologist Margaret Mead and the physicist J. Robert Oppenheimer) who begin as academics, most Influencers are not particularly gifted in disciplinary study and do not like school. They are seen as youths of talent and energy who lack a clear sense of where they are going to end up.

Influencers favor certain intelligences. They need to be gifted in language, particularly spoken language, because of the importance of storytelling. Either this talent unfolds in a natural way, as occurred with future university president Robert Maynard Hutchins, or it must be worked on compulsively, as happened with Winston Churchill. A gift for written language is also welcome, though less essential, except for those who aspire to exert influence in an indirect manner. The capacity to confront fundamental questions about life—recently dubbed existential intelligence—is also valued.

The other area of strength inheres in the realm of personal intelligence. It is vital that Influencers understand other individuals: what motivates them, how to work cooperatively with them if possible, how to manipulate them if necessary. High

IQs are no help in this matter. (As if to underscore this point, studies of political leaders have revealed that the most charismatic have little understanding of economic issues.) Finally, a shrewd sense of oneself—one's sometimes changing goals, strengths, weaknesses, and needs—is an important ingredient for the successful Influencer.

Perhaps the most striking feature in the biographies of Influencers is their willingness, often from a very young age, to challenge authority, to take risks in order to achieve their goals. Emblematic in this sphere was future General of the Army George C. Marshall. By inclination an unobtrusive individual, Marshall was nonetheless fearless in asserting himself. When barely twenty years of age, he barged into the office of then President William McKinley and urged that he be allowed to take an examination so that he could be commissioned as a second lieutenant. The first time he met General Pershing, head of the Allied Expeditionary Forces in the First World War, he criticized him publicly; shortly thereafter Marshall was named Pershing's principal aide. And the first time Marshall found himself at a small meeting with President Franklin D. Roosevelt, he took the risk of disagreeing aloud with the president. Then Secretary of the Treasury Henry Morgenthau quipped to Marshall at the end of the meeting, "Well, it's been nice knowing you." But true to form, Marshall was invited to become Army Chief of Staff just a few months later.

In most cases, so far as I can ascertain, these confrontations are not set up just to parade one's keen judgment. Nor is the future Influencer unnecessarily abrasive. Rather, it seems that E. I. truly believes he has mastered the facts of a matter and can contribute substantively to its resolution. Something pushes him over the edge and he speaks up, thereby risking his position in the group. We of course cannot know about those individuals whose public challenges result in banishment or death. But a sense that one is an equal, that one is somehow authorized to express one's deep beliefs, emerges as an important early marker of the individual who will eventually come to occupy positions of authority.

Coming to positions of power is one thing, bringing about

lasting change quite another. Only those aspiring Influencers who can create powerful stories and engage the minds and spirits of followers will be able to convert power into Influence.

We do not find analogous cases of public confrontation in the early lives of Makers and Masters. But we may find the functional equivalent—a challenge of orthodoxy through one's work. Whether it is Freud ignoring traditional views of hysteria, children, and dreams; or Virginia Woolf scuttling plot and character development in favor of an exploration of conscious experience, the Maker ends up at odds with the ideas and practices of others in a domain. And when their own innovations come to be accepted as the conventional wisdom, they place themselves "at risk" for being toppled by the next generation of iconoclastic creators.

Let me mention some other early markers. Influencers cut their teeth in local circles: their family, their group of friends, their schoolmates. The diameter of these circles rapidly expands, so that the Influencer finds herself dealing with hundreds if not thousands of individuals. It is important that the Influencer come to know the minds of these individuals, for their reactions will determine the effectiveness of his message. Influencers often crave different experiences, roaming the world to behold diverse sights and remote cultures. (Oddly, aspiring tyrants refrain from travel, perhaps not wanting to complexify their own views of the world—or risk a coup in their absence!) Unless the future Influencer is working in an art or a science, there is no need to master a traditional domain. And yet, very much like creators, E. I. must spend a decade or so learning about the political realm—or a major neighboring route to influence, such as journalism, the military, or business.

Many Influencers, particularly those in the political or religious realm, have lost a parent (typically a father) when they are young. Many others, including recent American presidents Clinton, Reagan, and Nixon, have fathers who were ineffectual. In the absence of a strong male parental figure, these Influencers are stimulated to create a set of norms, an overall ideology, of their own. This decision does not by any means translate into a benign philosophy; indeed, as many tyrants as saints have lost a parent at a tender age. However, early loss of one or both parents does mean that the story eventually created by the Influencer is more likely to be his *own* story, reflecting his own circumstances and his own identity—rather than a saga inherited or borrowed from others.

In nearly every particular, Mahatma (born Mohandas) Gandhi reflects the pattern of Influencers, of direct leaders. He was born in 1869 in Porbandar on the Arabian Sea. His family was not wealthy but had been engaged in public service for several generations. Gandhi was not a particularly good student and did not like school. As he once declared: "I am an average man with less than an average ability. I admit that I am not sharp intellectually. But I do not mind. There is a limit to the development of the intellect but none of that of the heart" (quoted in Nanda, 1985, p. 133). His family was immersed in moral issues, and young Gandhi himself spent much time weighing issues of right and wrong. He remonstrated himself for many years even for trivial infractions. Gandhi felt especially guilty about the fact that, while still a young teenager, he had left the bedside of his ailing father in order to have sexual relations with his equally young bride. When Gandhi returned to his father's room, his father had died. From here on, Gandhi, like other future leaders, was on his own ethically—he had to establish his own code of behavior.

Gandhi openly defied norms by going to England to study the law; this decision led to his virtual banishment from his native community. In London, Gandhi was a relatively lonely and awkward person who did not fit in to the more sophisticated culture. Passing (like Freud) through an extended psychosocial moratorium, Gandhi experimented with various cultural and ideological forms during his three years in Britain. Signs that he was not afraid to confront authority also surfaced in England; when one Dr. Allinson was propounding a set of practices that Gandhi himself found abhorrent, Gandhi nonetheless defended his associate against those peers who were attempting to banish the hapless Allinson from a group to which they all belonged. Gandhi commented thereafter: "I found myself siding with the losing party. But I had comfort in the thought that the cause was right" (Gandhi, 1948, p. 54).

Gandhi returned to his native India in 1891, only to learn that his mother had just died. At the time he intended to pursue a traditional legal career. A crucial turning point occurred when Gandhi was unexpectedly handed the chance to go to South Africa. Despite the fact that he had a young and growing family, Gandhi seized the opportunity to travel to another remote part of the world and, ultimately, to be an actor on a stage much wider than his home province.

In South Africa, Gandhi discovered that his fellow Indians were being treated as second-class citizens. Even affluent Indians were not allowed to sit in the first-class compartments of trains or to stay in good hotels. Given his keen sense of justice, Gandhi became increasingly distraught. As he recalled: "I thus made an intimate study of the hard conditions of the Indian settlers, not only by reading and hearing about it, but by personal experience. I saw that South Africa was no country for a self-respecting Indian and my mind became more and more occupied with the question as to how that state of thing[s] might be improved" (quoted in Brown, 1989, p. 32).

In South Africa, Gandhi slowly forged the elements of resistance that he was to perfect many years later in India. This required the honing of his linguistic and his personal skills— sometimes with the inspiration of others, sometimes by lonely self-study and experimentation. Over the course of a decade or more, he learned to express himself expertly in English, both orally and in writing. He gained a facility for sizing up individuals whose support he could count on—be they Indian, British, or Afrikaaner—and those who were not to be trusted.

Often Gandhi placed himself at risk. In 1897 he was beaten almost into unconsciousness by a white mob on the streets of Durban. Characteristically he felt sorry for the ignorant individuals who had attacked him and did not press charges. In 1908 he was jailed for the first time. He began to experiment with the practices of satyagraha—searching for common ground, refraining from violence, and allowing himself to be peacefully arrested. During his final years in South Africa, sickened by racist South African laws, Gandhi became significantly more confrontational: he burned his registration certificate publicly; he led protest marches in which thousands of individuals functioned as an army of peace; he sought to fill the jails with his compariots.

Gandhi was strengthened—indeed, formed—by these experiences. Confrontations with hard reality strengthened his resolve. In ever-widening circles, Gandhi came to be respected as a man of honor and a person who could accomplish much without generating hostility.

Gandhi underwent changes of an intensely personal sort. He found that it was not sufficient for him to be a man of means, with property, influence, and a large family. He felt the need to remake himself spiritually. Abandoning a busy home and professional life in Johannesburg, Gandhi moved with his wife and four sons to a farm called Phoenix House at the outskirts of Durban. Gandhi simplified his life consciously. He immersed himself in issues of health and medical care. He performed daily exercises and prepared his own food. And then in 1910 he founded Tolstoy Farm—a collection of people drawn from different religions and regions of India. Residents lived as members of a joint family in an ascetic, cooperative, and morally exemplary fashion. Gandhi felt he could not proceed as an ethical agent, seeking a better life for his people, unless he had himself attained and come to embody moral authority. He had to purify himself before he could make demands of others.

Gandhi returned to his native India at the start of 1915. At the time he was a virtual stranger, having spent most of the previous twenty-six years abroad. By agreement with his mentor, Gopal Krishna Gokhale, Gandhi refrained from speaking publicly during the first year back home. Instead, armed with a third-class railway coach ticket, he toured India, familiarizing himself with conditions and evaluating the courses of actions that he (and his followers) might pursue in the years to come. The experiments carried out in South Africa, and the results of Gandhi's survey of his own land, led to plans for social protest that Gandhi activated in Ahmedabad, Bardoli, and many other sites throughout India during the last thirty years of his life.

Stories and the Unschooled Mind

An Exemplary Influencer creates a story and must be able to connect with an audience that will help him to realize that story. This dialectic aspect sharply distinguishes Influencers from Makers. Until the time of her breakthrough, the Maker must wrestle chiefly with materials in the domain, with the symbol systems devised by earlier practitioners, in order to capture important elements and configure them in a generative way. In contrast, the Influencer—the architect of the leading story—must ever be in contact with other human beings, trying out the story, making adjustments, monitoring their reactions, and repeating this cycle indefinitely. The story must be sufficiently novel to generate interest, yet not so original as to defy credibility. And if they want the story to have lasting impact, Influencers must create or take over an organization that will help make the new story remain alive in the psyches of their followers.

Gandhi faced challenges in both of these respects. He did not begin by envisioning the minds of Indians and British as blank slates. On the contrary, he knew that each group adhered to flagrant and largely negative stereotypes—the Indians saw the British as swaggering bullies, who suppressed any nascent signs of nationalism; the British saw the Indians as weak and ineffectual individuals, clearly incapable of governing themselves. Additionally, Gandhi could not count on an already organized mass either in South Africa or in India. Instead, he had to cobble together an organization—actually *many* organizations—in both sites and find ways to keep them together. As we've seen, this process did not always work—for instance, an organization held in Ahmedabad but not in Chauri Chaura.

For new stories to prevail, they must defeat the already existing stories—which I have termed *counterstories*. Effective Influencers purvey stories that compete successfully with the many counterstories that already inhabit the mind of an audience. If one's audience is sophisticated and shares many common experiences, then the Influencer can afford to tell a story that is both novel and complicated; such is the privilege of Makers who work in relatively circumscribed domains. But if, as is usually the case with major Influencers, they are seeking to work with a distinctly heterogeneous group, then their story must be one that can be grasped by the unschooled mind.

A classic and powerful story that speaks to the unschooled mind is the Manichaean story—the struggle between good and evil. Many Influencers are quite successful in creating two groups (us and them); in fostering conflict between the two groups; and in rallying the members of "us" to prevail over "them." In briefest form, this is the story that British Prime Minister Margaret Thatcher related to great effect—her "individual entrepreneurial Tory story" was arrayed against the defeated, collectivist vision of Labor Socialist rivals. Other very simple stories are the Hitlerian story that "might is right" and the totalitarian story, "the nation is supreme."

It is possible to convey a more complex story, but this process takes a long period of time. The Influencer in this case becomes an educator, instructing his audience over time to think in a subtler manner. In my view Mahatama Gandhi attains heroic status precisely because he succeeded, over many years, in convincing thousands, perhaps millions, of individuals to think differently about the most important human issues.

In Gandhi's case, the unschooled counterstories were all too familiar: depending on your perspective, the strong (or bullying) British, the weak (or noble) Indians. Based on such simplistic analyses, all assumed that the struggle would eventually have to be engaged violently—with English arms and prestige being arrayed against Indian numbers and nationalistic zeal. Gandhi succeeded in convincing people the world over to reconceptualize matters: one should not judge people by the color of their skin or the history of their forebears but rather as fellow human beings; it is possible to have disagreements in a nonviolent way; and, most stirringly, both parties in a conflict can be strengthened if they handle themselves with dignity in the course of nonviolent confrontations. In our own time, Nelson Mandela has followed a similar path.

It may seem, a priori, that it is preferable to have an inclusionary story over an exclusionary story. That is, the broader the sense of "we," the more likely that the Influencer will be supported and ultimately achieve his mission. This may be true to a point; after all, if no one feels "at one" with the Influencer, he is not likely to be effective. However, there are unexpected costs to an overly inclusive "we." When the tent becomes too large, individuals who once felt special no longer experience a unique link to the leader; they become disaffected and present themselves as prime targets for the appeal of a new (and contrary) leader. It is telling in this regard that Mahatama Gandhi was assassinated not by a rival Muslim but by a member of his own Hindu group—a fate similar to that met in 1995 by Israeli Prime Minister Yitzhak Rabin.

I have written of "story creation" as a conscious process; and, indeed, much weaving of narratives is indeed intentional, particularly in a period of "image makers" and "spin doctors." Yet Influencers are unlikely to achieve success unless their story is genuine, one that grows naturally out of their own experiences and touches the lived experiences of their audience. At least some of this communication occurs at an unconscious level; and the story cannot be dissociated from its vivid teller, be it the simply clad Gandhi or the bulldog-like Churchill.

The Ultimate Campaign

The events in Ahmedabad and Chauri Chaura were but early skirmishes in a much grander campaign. Gandhi wanted to convince the whole world that India must be allowed to move gradually but inexorably to full independence. It may not be possible to pick a moment when this point was brought home to the world, but the salt march of 1930 is as plausible a candidate as any. The march was triggered by the imposition in India of a tax on salt, a measure widely perceived as unfair and regressive in a society where that condiment is literally a matter of life and death.

On March 12, 1930, Gandhi and a small group of followers began a 200-mile journey from Ahmedabad, heading toward the coast. The crowd grew in size each day, finally reaching nearly 2 miles in length, as individuals at each site along the way were convinced to join in a symbolic act of protest: the picking up of salt from the sea. This action was a technical violation of the law, for any participant was thereby making salt from seawater rather than paying a tax on legally manufactured salt. In an action deliberately modeled after the famous Boston Tea Party, Gandhi said in effect, Punish us for carrying out a reasonable action and show the world what you are really like; or, by repealing this unfair law, show the world what you could be like—and we will do the same.

At first, in the absence of a governmental response to Gandhi's act of civil disobedience, there was a slight feeling of anticlimax among the marchers. But soon protests mounted all over India. In the words of Jawaharlal Nehru, Gandhi's long-time political ally, "it seemed as though a spring had been suddenly released" (quoted in Bondurant, 1958, p. 94). Gandhi was arrested, along with many others involved in the campaign. Then in a dramatic confrontation, the policemen near the Dharasana Salt Works openly attacked a file of disciplined satyagrahis. The satyagrahis did not respond in kind: instead, they simply took the blows to their heads and bodies and eventually fell to the ground. In a famous dispatch, Webb Miller, a reporter from the United Press, informed the world: "there was no fight, no struggle; the marchers simply walked forward till struck down. The police commenced to savagely kick the seated men in the abdomen and testicles and then dragged them by their arms and feet and throw them into the ditches" (quoted in Shirer, 1979, p. 98). Finally, the British broke the rebellion but at a dear cost: the moral hold that Britain had presumed to exert over India had been permanently shattered.

After such bloodshed, it was only a matter of time until the British dominion over India collapsed and India became a free nation. No doubt this process was sped up by the Second World War: fighting for its own survival, Britain had little energy left to continue to assert itself over the Indian subcontinent. Indeed, in the end, the chief conflicts occurred not between Great Britain and a united India but rather between the Hindu and Muslim populations of India, with the Hindus calling for a single nation, the Muslims insistent on partition. This internecine struggle actually led to the very bloodshed that Gandhi had devoted his life to eradicate. The cruelest irony was that, only months after independence, Gandhi was assassinated while approaching a prayer ground by a Hindu extremist (Nathuram Vinayak Godse).

Dealing with Failure

Individuals fail all the time, and as individuals with huge agendas (and comparably sized egos), Influencers stand at special risk for failure. Indeed, all the leaders I studied experienced many failures or defeats, some distinctly minor, others quite daunting. At the age of thirty, Stalin and Hitler were nonentities, and any notion that they were shortly to become world leaders would have sounded ludicrous. Mao Zedong lost almost his entire base of support when he was in his thirties. If the Second World War had not broken out, their countrymen would never have turned to Winston Churchill or Charles de Gaulle; and their brief biographies would have sadly noted the disjunction between their formidable talents and the modest mark they left on the world scene. For every successful campaign, Gandhi could list ones that failed in one or another respect, often leaving human casualties in their wake.

Leaders fail for many reasons. They are not as convincing as they aspire to be, the circumstances are not right, a rival (or associate) seizes the moment. Often they overreach themselves, and are countered by reactionary factors. Some, like Margaret Thatcher, constantly tempt fate, ever pushing the envelope further, until the edifice they have constructed comes tumbling down. Followers are not always grateful, particularly to people who have made them stretch too far: both Churchill and de Gaulle found themselves out of office just after the Second World War. Indeed, larger-than-life figures often leave in their wake mediocre figures, who either are content just to rest on the laurels of their predecessors or who slowly dismantle the more awesome of the creations of the formidable Influencer.

Gandhi was fortunate that Free India was led by the highly capable Nehru; but thereafter, India has been governed by a string of noninspiring individuals, who have succeeded in dissipating much of the Gandhi-Nehru legacy. Gandhi may have exerted more of an impact on other societies—South Africa, the United States during the Civil Rights movement—than on his own.

I have been struck by how Influencers themselves deal with failure. Influencers do not treat a setback as an occasion to give up—indeed, they are unlikely to see a defeat as failure at all. Rather, they are embattled, energized, and posed to throw themselves back into the fray with new force. Richard Nixon, no stranger to losses, saw his life as a series of crises to which he had to respond. He repeatedly emphasized that a person is never defeated when he loses, but only when he ceases to struggle.

No one has made this point more pithily than Jean Monnet, who encountered more than his share of setbacks in the sixty-plus years that he pushed for a united Europe. Monnet said: "I regard every defeat as an opportunity." Henry Ford reflected that "failure is the opportunity to begin again more intelligently." Indeed, I have discovered similar sayings in the speeches and writings of nearly every Influencer I have studied.

In this respect Gandhi is exemplary. He recognized his failures—he referred famously to one as a "Himalayan blunder" (Gandhi, 1948, p. 424)—but never let any of them deter him from pursuing the course of action in which he wholeheartedly believed. Instead, he saw his life as solely a set of "experiments with truth . . . such experiments are an integral part of my life; they are essential for my mental peace and self-realization" (1948, p. vii). He reflected on each episode, learned from it, shared what he learned with all who would listen, and then plunged again into the thick of the matter, often with renewed vigor. "I have found by experience," he told his readers, "that man makes his plans to be often upset by God, but at the same time when the ultimate goal is the search of truth, no matter how a man's plans are frustrated, the issue is never injurious and often better than anticipated" (1948, p. 270). Gandhi resolutely accepted the suffering of the satyagrahi: "A satyagrahi differs from the generality of men in that, if he submits to a restriction, he submits voluntarily not because he is afraid of punishment, but because he thinks such submission is essential to the common weal" (quoted in Fischer, 1983, p. 85). Sentenced to six years in jail, Gandhi showed how he could frame setbacks in a constructive manner. Without irony, he declared to Lord Broomfield, the presiding judge: "So far as the sentence is concerned, I certainly consider that it is as light as any judge could inflict on me and so far as the whole proceedings are concerned, I must say that I could not have expected greater courtesy" (quoted in Payne, 1990, p. 367).

Influencers may differ from the rest of us, then, not in their proportion of defeats but, rather, in the way they construe their own losses. When events spin out of control, they do not conclude that they are unfit for the position or that the cause is unjust. Rather, they succeed in so framing the situation that it reconstitutes as an opportunity from which they (and their followers) can draw lessons. They may be aided by the phenomenon of *cognitive dissonance*: in the aftermath of a setback, their devoted followers often feel more, rather than less, committed. And they are encouraged to reflect, to plan anew, and, so reinvigorated, to advance. Gandhi, indeed, seemed to take special pleasure in relating efforts that had failed, and in reflecting on the lessons that could be learned from them: "it is by my sorrows that I can soar," he liked to remark (quoted in Brown, 1989, p. 381). In societies that have undergone difficult times, the heroes are often those who persevere despite the apparent lack of success in the mundane world—quite possibly, because they believe that these efforts will be crowned with glory in an afterlife.

Just as Influencers are not deterred—are, in fact, spurred on—by failure, they are rarely satisfied by success. Their goals are high, and they are often energized by the struggle rather than by the outcome. They may prefer to see themselves as embattled, even isolated, rather than as uncritically adulated. Both Thomas Jefferson and Mao Zedong called for a revolution every generation—presumably because they feared that satisfaction with the status quo would mask a loss of ardor or spur a regression to the mediocre mean. Gandhi stated of his experiments: "I claim for them nothing more than does a scientist who never claims any finality about his conclusions, but keeps an open mind regarding them" (1948, p. viii). It is scarcely an exaggeration to state that all Influencers fail in their ultimate mission; what invigorates them is the nobility of their effort, and the hope—more strongly, the conviction—that they will have left some kind of enduring imprint on future lives.

EIGHT

Varieties of Extraordinariness

Taking Stock

Were this a book in the humanities, it would end about here. The humanistic scholar seeks detailed understanding of the individual in his or her fullness. Even a rough typology of four extraordinary figures extends beyond the humanist's customary brief.

Like the humanistic scholar, I revel in the specifics of Mozart, Freud, Woolf, and Gandhi. But as a psychologist (and social scientist), I seek to understand these individuals not only in themselves but as representatives of the diverse ways in which individuals can excel. And to the extent possible, I want to anticipate other forms of extraordinariness, determine which patterns may exist there, and, ultimately, understand the options pursued by those who become extraordinary.

In the opening chapters of this book, I introduced the categorical schemes that underlie my approach to extraordinariness.

These were largely left aside during my examination of four individuals—and perhaps this deliberate bracketing made for smoother reading. But it is now time to draw upon these schemes as we seek to comprehend the broader terrain of extraordinariness.

Of the distinctions introduced, three prove most crucial. First of all, there is the distinction between an interest in the domains of accomplishment that exist in one's society and an interest in the human beings who populate the society. A primary thrust toward domains of knowledge is quite different from one directed toward the realm of human beings; this distinctive proclivity emerges early in life and endures throughout life. Our first two types—Mozart and Freud—were described in terms of their relationship to domains: Mozart as a student of the art of music, Freud as a student of the science of psychology. Our latter two types were described in terms of their relationship to human beings: Woolf turned inward to herself, Gandhi reached out to other individuals.

A second distinction concerns one's stance toward revolution within a domain. This distinction emerges clearly in the comparison between Mozart and Freud. As a Master (and, earlier, as a prodigy), Mozart was intent on realizing the most powerful work within established genres; like Keats, Tolstoy, and George Eliot, he is known for bringing a domain to its culminating form. As a Maker, Freud sampled the various domains in his society but found them wanting; satisfaction came only when he had essentially created a new domain, within which he and his collaborators could work and ultimately be judged. The distinction between "acceptance" and "overthrow" of a domain proves less acute in the realm of persons. But both Woolf and Gandhi are best seen as innovators here: whatever their initial points of departure, Woolf (unlike Eliot) challenged the current practices of the novel, while Gandhi (unlike Thatcher) introduced new political forms.

We may say, then, that extraordinary individuals make two choices, more or less consciously: whether to focus on persons or on objects, and whether to invest in the perfection of domain practices or attempt to overthrow them.

A third distinction concerns the way creativity and other

forms of extraordinariness have been conceived in this work. It has been standard practice, in both psychology and lay terms, to place creativity solely inside the head of the creative individual—she is creative; he is not. However, thanks to the reconceptualization brought about by Csikszentmihalyi, we now construe creativity as emerging from the dynamics among three different elements: the *person* with his or her talents; the *domain* in which work is carried out; and the judgments wrought by the surrounding *field* of judges.

Additional leverage may be gained by extending this triad as follows. The individual is seen as the starting point for a node that includes family and local community; the domain is seen as the starting point for a node that includes the range of cultural forms; the field is seen as the starting point for a node that encompasses the wider society. And all three nodes overlap as one focuses on the individual in his or her primary relation to work. A more nuanced diagram emerges:

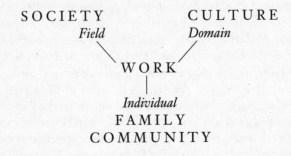

These distinctions allow social scientists to make contact with large bodies of theory and research—say, with what is known about the family and the larger culture. They are relevant as well in a general treatise because they help us to identify forms of extraordinariess that might not have otherwise been recognized, and to appreciate the relationships among the various types that have been introduced here.

Let me cite a few examples. A prodigy like Mozart emerges as an individual who happens to have a talent that fits very closely to an existing domain; indeed, there may have been a preordained fit between Mozart's mind and the classical music of his era. The talents of a Maker like Freud are more suited to a domain that remains to be discovered and a field that is yet to be constituted. Virginia Woolf emerges as an individual with a special interest in the world of persons, both in her immediate family and, eventually, her peers in Bloomsbury; at the same time, she is at first a Master of writing and then, increasingly, a Maker of new genres. She helps to create a field that savors women writers. Gandhi's interest also centers on the world of persons, but it extends beyond family and community to the wider society. Like Woolf, he achieves some of his effect indirectly, through the creation of powerful written symbols; but he transcends such literary forms in his direct relations with others, his embodiment of a certain set of principles, and his willingness to engage in high-stakes public performances.

Again I must stress that these distinctions are not absolute. Nearly all extraordinary individuals exhibit more than one form of excellence—Freud may be seen as realizing all four in some measure. He—and his doting parents—would have been pleased by this accomplishment. Most extraordinary persons also exhibit weaknesses: Mozart was not particularly introspective, and Freud's mastery of physical science and mathematics was uneven. Some figures also overlap our distinctions. Thus Freud's chosen domain entailed knowledge about human beings. The distinctions are best thought of as helpful guides, not as a mutually exclusive categorical system.

Armed with the above distinctions, one may envision a plethora of forms of extraordinariness. Without striving to be comprehensive, I consider here several additional forms that help to flesh out our picture of the unusual and the notable. I then reflect on some of the issues raised by this line of study. Lessons are drawn in the concluding chapter of the book.

Fame and Success

If one reviews the lists of the best-known individuals within a society, particularly a media-drenched society like the United States's, one finds great changes from one decade to another. As I write in the mid-1990s, figures such as the performance artist Madonna, the figure skater Nancy Kerrigan, and the media personality Howard Stern top the lists. It is unlikely that these people will remain prominent.

I speak here about *celebrity*, defined by some wag as individuals who are famous for being famous. The visual artist Andy Warhol predicted that in our time everyone would be famous for fifteen minutes. Whatever its departure from literal reality, this phrase captures an provocative insight. The media are always scanning for the unusual, and our individual forms of unusualness—voluntary or inadvertent—can conspire to make any of us known for a time. Moreover, those of us who either want lasting fame or can exploit momentary glory are sometimes able to remain in the limelight—most typically, today, by appearing on a regular television show, advertising a product, or starting a franchise business.

Fame and success are closely allied, but they are not identical. *Fame* generally means that an individual has come to the attention of particular fields or of the larger society. There is no need for an individual talent, no need for a contribution to a domain. *Success* generally equates with the acquisition of material resources (or, more rarely, some kind of prestige) through a deliberate, legitimate effort (rather than, say, through luck or illegal activities). A person achieves success when he or she is rewarded for a contribution to a domain.

Various relations obtain between fame and success. Many business people are extremely successful, but they either revel in or at least accept their anonymity. And there are certainly individuals who attain momentary fame—for example, someone who saves a person from drowning—who are discovered years later to be living in poverty. Our media culture tends to merge the famous and the successful: if you become famous, there are opportunities to acquire material rewards; and if you become one of the richest people in the world, a spotlight is likely to be cast upon you by virtue of your assets alone.

Celebrity or fame does not preclude genuine creativity or leadership but cannot be confused with it. A creative individual must change a domain. Only if the domain of performance artistry is significantly altered on account of Madonna's contributions does she become a candidate for being creative. It is salutary to acknowledge the temporal dimensions of human accomplishment. For most of his years, the contemporary painter Harold Shapinsky toiled in obscurity. But when demand arose for abstract expressionist paintings of a certain vintage, Shapinsky's work suddenly became valued; it was not the works that had changed, but rather the requirements of the broader society.

Spiritual Extraordinariness

So far I have focused primarily on individuals who can influence others by the quality and originality of their works. But there exists another powerful form of influence, in which the very presence of an individual affects those with whom that person comes into contact. I call this "spiritual extraordinariness."

I became sensitized to this issue through my studies of Mahatma Gandhi and Pope John XXIII. Something about the physical being of these individuals affected others. For many people, proximity to Gandhi was itself an experience of riveting importance, of unforgettable personal influence. Much the same can be said about other Influencers like John XXIII, Martin Luther King, Jr., and Mother Teresa, or about artistic performers such as Yo-Yo Ma, Pablo Casals, Janis Joplin, and Jimi Hendrix. Such charismatic individuals stimulate others to alter their consciousness and, perhaps, to change their modes of living.

Moreover, unfortunately, such power is not restricted to those who have benign impulses: cult leaders like David Koresh and the Reverend Jimmy Jones, and nationalist leaders like

Hitler, Mao Zedong, and Muramar Qaddafi, also exert a spiritual hold over many followers.

Which features contribute to power over others? Often the leader's striking physical appearance, combined with hypnotic powers, convince listeners that they are being spoken to directly, powerfully, singularly. The charismatic leader exudes charm and energy; the follower believes that he can imbibe some of this essence if he remains in the vicinity of the spiritual individual. An apparent dynamic is at work: the follower not only loves the spiritual figure but believes that the love is requited. Probably all of us have the potential at times to fall under the sway of such a luminous figure; clearly some of us are especially prone to the formation of such deeply affecting ties.

Clearly a cult leader like David Koresh or an exotic guru like Georgei Gurdjieff is an Influencer, extremely knowledgeable about the manipulation of others. But rather than being oriented toward some external goal—for example, bringing about social change—the central mission of such gurus is a "cult of personality": an attempt to suppress the "enthusiast's" own individuality by merging it with the consciousness of the omniscient spiritual figure. As noted psychiatrist Anthony Storr points out, there is no genuine interplay between the consciousness of cult leader and follower: the individual with spiritual power is completely immersed in her own psyche. Thus, Influencing occurs in the service of Introspection: an effort to substitute one's own concerns, one's personal world view, for those of the other individuals within one's orbit.

Note that this capacity to move others significantly need not be divorced from other forms of extraordinariness. There are individuals—Margaret Mead and Robert Oppenheimer among them—whose ideas are so incandescent that they deeply affect individuals who value intellectual power. Indeed, it may be difficult to gain spiritual hegemony over others in the absence of any messages or ideas; and sometimes, as in the case of Gandhi, the spiritual power grows out of a convincing narrative. But the ideas are not primary in the case of the guru—they are mere means for seducing others.

Moral Extraordinariness

As a scholar who investigates extraordinariness, I am often asked about the morality of my subjects. The questions have a "damned if you do, damned if you don't" quality: sometimes I am berated for studying only individuals whom I admire, while at other times I am criticized for studying individuals who are less than admirable.

Both critiques miss the thrust of my undertaking. The models I'm developing should be applicable to *all* Masters, Makers, Influencers, and Introspectors, independent of their moral merits; at the same time, the models should help us to understand those individuals who do not qualify—for example, people who are famous or successful but who do not ultimately affect others.

One can judge a pattern of behavior as moral, amoral, or immoral only if one is informed about the context in which that thought or action takes place. To be sure, certain values—like love of one's children, honesty in personal dealings, or respect for the sanctity of human life—receive almost universal approbation. Yet one can envision circumstances under which these values would have to contest with contrasting values—love of one's country, need to protect someone from knowledge that would hurt him, the urgency of getting rid of a tyrant—that seem equally pressing.

Within a given cultural context, it is possible to cordon off a moral domain and to consider individuals in terms of their extraordinariness in that sphere. Developmental psychologists Anne Colby and William Damon have identified Americans who undertook activities of enormous caring—for example, adopting many foster children or devoting their lives to the alleviation of hunger or the preservation of the environment.

These moral exemplars stood out in a number of respects. They believed passionately in what they were doing and had no doubts that they were pursuing the proper course of action. They were overwhelmingly positive in attitude, believing that setbacks were only temporary or part of a larger plan. Their beliefs were often founded on a religious basis. Perhaps surprisingly, they did not regard what they were doing as anything special—they assumed, we might say naively, that anyone else in their position would behave with equal nobility. Their scores on standard tests of moral reasoning did not stand out—the capacity to behave in a caring way seems quite different than the capacity to reason acutely about moral dilemmas.

These remarkably selfless behaviors and attitudes are best explained through a long-term developmental perspective: over time, these individuals established habits that led them to devote their lives to serving their fellow human beings. And, inspiringly, they saw service to others as part of their own personal growth.

It is instructive to compare such moral exemplars to the extraordinary individuals examined in these pages. For the most part I would not term them creative, for (unlike Gandhi or Freud) they rarely devised novel ways of helping others: they merely took seriously the practices recommended since time immemorial by Influencers like Christ. Though they affected individuals around them, most of this influence was quite local; thus they qualify as influencers only with a small *i*. To the extent that they inspired others to undertake comparable good works, these individuals earn the descriptor *spiritual*.

The distinctions introduced in this study can help illuminate morality. Individuals may behave morally, immorally, or amorally in any domain of activity that they master; they may give forth a similar range of contributions in cases where they "make" a new domain. Their behaviors toward others may be similarly varied. Perhaps the "moral exemplar" is most singular in the extent to which he sacrifices his personal goals for those of his family, the broader community, or even world society. Knowledge of self or other, interests in a domain of knowledge or skill, are harnessed to a broader concern: the improvement of life conditions for those other than oneself. Of course, this goal is sometimes delusional; and that is why—as in the case of creativity—one requires some version of a "field" before one can render reliable judgments about who or what "counts" as moral.

The survival of our culture, indeed our world civilization, may depend more upon the morality of citizens than upon their making, their influencing, or their spirituality. Ralph Waldo Emerson remarked famously, "Character is higher than intellect" (quoted in Coles, 1997). Struggles among civilizations as often turn on moral considerations as on issues of economics or political hegemony. Yet, because such considerations cannot be undertaken apart from the ethics and values of particular societies, they cannot be approached in the same way as the forms of extraordinariness on which I have focused here.

Extraordinary Deviations

When one speaks of extraordinariness, there may be a tendency to focus on the high end of the bell-shaped curve: on those individuals and institutions representing the most formidable accomplishments. Our understanding is enhanced, however, when we examine individuals who stand out because of differences or deficiencies. Moreover, as the concept of fruitful asynchrony intimates, the combination of powers *and* deficits sometimes turns out to be productive.

Dating back to the classical figure of the archer Philoctetus, Western societies have pondered the relation between the wound and the bow. As the price of the gift of creation, it is argued, individuals must suffer from a defect, some kind of initial or acquired wound. Certainly, there is no difficulty in documenting the many artists who have physical defects (the lame Byron, the deaf Beethoven) or psychic trauma (the neglected Brontë sisters, the schizophrenic Robert Schumann). But because many creators lack such obvious defects, and because the possession of such defects does not itself assure extraordinariness, one can at most identify correlations—à la Virginia Woolf—between kinds of wounds and kinds of accomplishment.

Certain wounds recur in the lives of extraordinary individuals. Prominent is the loss, during early childhood, of one or both parents. Writer Jean-Paul Sartre once remarked that the best gift a father can give his son is to die young. Ignoring the hyperbole and the irony, it does seem that the sustaining of an early loss motivates individuals to create a world that is more perfect in their imagination; on more occasions than would have occurred by chance, such invention has culminated in a life of creativity or leadership. Should there be more than one major youthful trauma, the growing individual becomes increasingly at risk. One has the feeling that Virginia Woolf was initially wounded, and eventually defeated, by an accumulation of traumas. Clearly, certain traumas are sufficiently devastating that an individual's potential for accomplishment is shattered. One thinks in this context of the survivors of the Holocaust or of the Chinese Cultural Revolution, many of whom have been rendered incapable of productive work.

A neurological condition called temporal lobe epilepsy seems associated with creativity of a very different sort. A manifestation of this disorder, which entails seizures in the parts of the brain involved with language and emotion, is a tendency to write a great deal (*hypergraphia*) and to concentrate on religious themes (*hyperreligiosity*). In most cases of the "temporal lobe epilepsy personality," the individual behaves bizarrely in interpersonal relations; his or her copious writings are suffused with dramatic spiritual themes—of interest chiefly to the individual author and to those who study this syndrome. It has been claimed, however, that occasional artists afflicted with this syndrome, like Fyodor Dostoevsky and Vincent Van Gogh, reflect its peculiar world view in their artistic productions. In these instances, vivid forms of perception, secondary to pathology, may help to generate artistic work of unusual power.

When planning their political or religious campaigns or creating works of science or art, extraordinary individuals can focus their attention for many hours at a time, screening out even the most dissonant of stimuli. Such attention is desirable, of course, but it may be akin to autism—a pathological condition in which attention is so focused that the individual is unable ever to engage in normal human intercourse. It is not surprising that the incidence of autism is higher in the families of individuals who perform at a high level in certain academic disciplines, like mathematics, science, and engineering.

Marked focus is often accompanied by notable energy. Many

extraordinary individuals stay up for long hours, need little sleep, walk, run, or talk for much longer periods of time than do their peers—in fact, they often cannot function without outlets for the expenditure of their energy. And they often have voracious appetites—for experience, for food, for sex. We may assume that such generous allotments of energy are not simply an acquired capacity, though the potential to channel them toward one's work may be. And, like preternatural focus, they may relate, in ways yet to be discovered, to clinical conditions like hyperactivity or Tourette's syndrome.

Consider, finally, the apparent correlation between certain deficits and certain gifts. The neurologist Norman Geschwind and his close collaborator Albert Galaburda spoke of the "pathology of superiority." Specifically they proposed an intriguing syndrome featuring associations among left-hemisphere pathology in utero, linguistic problems, and a correlative flowering (more technically, hypertrophying) of spatial and artistic capacities. While their explanation of the syndrome remains controversial, Geschwind and Galaburda's general claim is consistent with our notion of fruitful asynchrony: a deficit in one cognitive or affective area may go hand-in-hand with the capacity to develop other kinds of strengths. Whether it be the loss of a parent, a rare neurological condition, or an unusual deployment of energy and attention, the sting of the wound can be transmuted into the string of the bow. One must *exploit* the asynchronies that have befallen one, link them to a promising issue or domain, reframe frustrations as opportunities, and, above all, persevere.

Peak Societies

Nearly all historians would concur that certain regions, in certain periods of history, have stood out in terms of the outstanding quality and quantity of accomplishments. Who would question the legitimacy of singling out Athens in the fifth century B.C., the Roman Empire at the time of Christ, the T'ang Dynasty in the eighth century, Islamic society in the late Middle Ages, the Italian city-states in the fifteenth century, France in the eighteenth century, the capitals of Central Europe at the turn of this century, or New York at the middle (and perhaps, once again, at the end) of our century?

It is possible to take a cynical view of these candidates, concluding that they answer some kind of a historians' need for consensual landmarks or merely reflect the random fluctuations of a historical barometer. I disagree. In my view, just as prodigies represent a unique confluence of personal, familial, domain, and historical consequences, so, too, "peak societies" represent a rare and difficult-to-sustain series of coincident events and forces.

As a prototype, consider Florence in the fifteenth century. Florence was pivotally located at the center of a number of thriving regions. Commerce through northern Italy was stunning, and people from all over the Mediterranean passed through these parts regularly. There was stimulating rivalry with other Italian regions, such as Venice, Siena, Milan, and Rome. Old arts and crafts were rediscovered even as new ones were burgeoning; the yearnings to explore new territories—geographical as well as scientific—were, after a millennium of quiescence, again on the rise.

In reaction to the somber mood of medieval times, there was a general religious and spiritual awakening—one turned toward outward celebration rather than hermetic contemplation. Perhaps as important, certain key families—particularly the Medicis—undertook to provide leadership (in both a constructive and a destructive sense) and served as patrons to the most outstanding creative figures, such as Ghiberti, da Vinci, Michelangelo, and Brunelleschi. One can discern early perturbations in this fecund region during the thirteenth and fourteenth centuries, a temporary height in the fifteenth century, and then a relatively rapid decline thereafter.

A similar story can be told about other "peak societies." There is a lively sense of activity that draws talented individuals to the center of the culture, arrays them in cooperation but also in competition, and supports the most evidently talented. The regime need not be democratic—in fact, a touch of authoritarianism may aid in the accomplishment of ambitious projects—

but there has to be some tolerance for the exploration of ideas and the testing of boundaries. A measure of affluence is essential. All four of our exemplary Masters partook of such rare historical confluences: Mozart absorbed energy from the Enlightenment; Freud drew on Viennese intellectual cross-currents; Woolf was inspired by the unique Bloomsbury circle; and Gandhi attempted to synthesize constructive themes of East and West during the early part of this century.

Peak societies are driven to excess, either in search of conquest abroad or as a consequence of celebration and waste at home. Vienna and London are no longer the apogees that they represented a century ago; New York, Tokyo, Berlin, or Rio de Janiero may someday be seen as passing through a similar cultural hegira during our own era. And just as a creative scientist or artist is eventually surpassed by an equally talented and hungrier younger colleague, so, too, the peak society eventually gives way to another that for a time occupies the forefront.

Societies may stand out in other respects. Egypt led for millennia in part by remaining absolutely constant. Confucian societies have survived precisely because they avoid meteoric rises and falls, and have placed little faith in scientific and technological advances per se. Dozens of Stone Age cultures endured with small numbers, over many centuries, through a kind of equilibrium with their ecology and their sometimes friendly, sometimes hostile neighbors. Native American societies, like the Keres Indians in New Mexico, harbor an entirely different view of giftedness—one that focuses on what one can contribute to the community. And, to pursue the pathology theme for a moment, some societies—the Ik portrayed by anthropologist Colin Turnbull, the Nazis under Hitler, the Soviet bloc of nations—have managed to decimate themselves in a brief span of time.

Questions

Even to undertake a study of extraordinariness is to invite questions. My focus on the individual-as-agent is bound to trouble some, particularly in this determinedly postmodern, interdisciplinary era. If the objection takes the form that there is much to be learned from focusing on cultural context and extrapersonal factors, I fully agree. Indeed, my discussion of the audience, my recognition of the domain and the field, represent efforts to introduce such elements into a realm of analysis that has been excessively psychological, even by a psychologist's standards.

And yet, just as it would be foolish to eliminate the biological or the cultural from a consideration of human nature, it seems misguided to attempt to eliminate, in Foucauldian or Lévi-Straussian fashion, the role and the agency of the individual. This book could be written from a less individualistic perspective; but, I submit, the individual would have to be smuggled in, one way or another, if the phenomena of interest are to be explicated. Mozart is not simply a better- (or worse-) behaved Antonio Salieri; Virginia Woolf's consciousness could not be easily replaced by those of Marcel Proust or Katherine Mansfield.

I have a positive motive for this focus. I believe that human beings cannot develop without some sense of possibility, some landmarks by which one can judge one's own growth or stagnation. By definition, we cannot all be extraordinary; but those who are extraordinary can help the rest of us understand our options, perils, and opportunities. Few would argue that one should study art without examining the greatest canvases, or that one should study science without mastering the most important theories and most telling empirical demonstrations. I agree with Nietzsche: "We must love and honor great individuals, and the tasks of scholars of the past is to bring such people constantly to the forefront of our minds" (quoted in Kaufmann, 1980). Does it make sense to continue on our life paths without having rich knowledge of the heights and the depths of which other human beings are capable?

Even if my project is fully granted, significant issues of method and bias must be engaged. I cannot assert that the approach here is scientific in any rigorous sense. For the most part, my studies are standard case studies, drawing on the published evidence about individuals, and in selected cases, on my own observations, interviews, and interactions with persons of outstanding accomplishment. Yet I claim to go beyond mere case studies—to approach science—in three senses.

First, my observations are grounded in knowledge that has been established through psychological and social science in the past century. Second, I am engaged in the construction of models—such as the Exemplary Maker or the Exemplary Influencer—that transcend individuals. Third, I am committed to empirical studies that can ferret out generalizations about various forms of extraordinariness. I could have reached for laws and tests right away. But I've concluded that our understanding of the laws—as well as the exceptions—that emerge will be significantly enhanced if we appreciate in fine detail the circumstances that lead to patterns in the first place.

To the charge that my study is time- and culture-bound, I plead guilty. For the most part, I have stuck to the modern era and to Western Culture; studies probing other times, places, and domains are needed. I also confess to a bias toward individuals whom I personally admire and from whom I have learned. And I admit that I have focused here on the benign sides of these individuals, rather than assuming the stance of the pathographer toward, say, Gandhi's behavior toward his family or Freud's treatment of his associates (and, at times, his data).

Yet I reject the notion that my conclusions apply only to positive exemplars. Each of my studies looks as well at less admirable individuals; and, as I have learned, there are no extraordinary individuals—not even saints!—who are not also sinners. Though morality is well worth studying, I have applied no moral litmus test in investigating individuals who have left marks on the persons and domains of their time.

A final critical comment features the assertion that it may be fascinating to read about the lives of the "intellectually rich and famous"; but that such a focus does not provide needed leverage on our own times, our own problems, our own lives. This critique may well have been apt with reference to my earlier studies. But I have always believed that all human beings can benefit from a better understanding of the islands of extraordinariness in our midst. In the concluding chapter, I turn explicitly to some such lessons.

NINE

Lessons

Is Extraordinariness Desirable?

Extraordinary individuals certainly make life more interesting. They add to our pleasure and our mental nourishment, though sometimes also to our travail. I find it intriguing to ask: Would you wish such a fate for yourself, your children, or others you care about?

Certainly there are rewards for extraordinariness—at times extraordinary people are treated as if they were important; perhaps more significantly, they come to feel that they have made a difference during their lifetimes and perhaps for posterity. But the costs of embarking on a life marked for extraordinariness are considerable.

To begin with, one must have enormous dedication to one's domain and one's mission. At a minimum, it takes ten years of steady application to master a domain; and thereafter, one must continue this concentrated work indefinitely if one is to keep up with advances.

The extraordinary individual is also perennially at risk for pain, rejection, and loneliness. Most innovators and most innovations are not well understood or appreciated at the time of their launching. The establishment is conservative, peers are jealous, the general public may be hostile. One needs thick skin to withstand the scrutiny that attends almost every breakthrough. Indeed, the aspirant for extraordinariness must prepare for a life in which the drums of criticism beat constantly. And while success may bring rewards, any triumph also ushers in a new round of jealousy and criticism . . . as well as the likelihood that one's ideas or works will be distorted, sometimes inadvertently, sometimes deliberately.

There are occasional extraordinary saints, as well as those rare achievers who maintain equilibrium in their lives. But the physics of extraordinariness pulls sharply in one direction. In general, as the end of life draws nearer, internal and external pressures direct extraordinary individuals to concentrate on their work to the exclusion of all else. Those associates and family members who are prepared to devote themselves to the pursuit of a mission are likely to remain in close contact with the extraordinary individual; but those who try to express their own views, or who are no longer seen as indispensable to the mission, are likely to be scuttled.

The lives of the extraordinary are often rimmed with casualties, some psychological, some mortal. Indeed, most of the extraordinary individuals I've studied have turned out to be very difficult people—often tortured, often inflicting suffering on those close to them. It is not uncommon for such extraordinary individuals to be personally unhappy, to undergo breakdowns, to feel suicidal, and to become estranged from close associates, who in turn may feel that their lives have been ruined. Even a moral titan like Gandhi proves no exception to this pattern, as his relations with his wife were marked by constant tension and his relation to his oldest son, Harilal, was an unmitigated disaster. Summarizing my dismaying conclusions on this topic, a British newspaper once ran the headline EINSTEIN = GENIUS MINUS NICENESS.

This portrait of the high price of extraordinariness should be leavened. First of all, while the extraordinary clearly lead demanding lives, it is not at all evident that their pains—and the pains they inflict on others—are worse than those associated with other select groups of individuals. (I wonder what the appropriate control group for extraordinariness would be.) Second, it is important to stress that extraordinary individuals are often capable of great acts of kindness and generosity—if they can be ogres at times, they may well be noble souls at other times.

Finally—and importantly—I do not feel that extraordinary individuals were fated from the first to become prickly persons. I doubt that they would stand out, at age twenty, on a psychologist's measure of "difficultness." Rather, their warped personalities grow out of their own, often tortured experiences. The extreme pressures of "going it alone" early in the career, combined with the enormous demands on them once they have "made it," conspire to make many of them eligible as subjects for a pathographical best-seller or film.

Contrasting Approaches: Formula or Atmosphere?

Despite such warning signals, many individuals (or their families) will choose—more or less consciously—to tackle the highest summits in a domain. It is probably the case, at least in our society, that the lust for material success is a stronger initial motivator than the desire to leave a permanent trace upon one's culture. I focus my remarks here, however, on those individuals who seek to play a role as a Maker or Master, an Influencer or Introspector.

Those who study accounts like this one for clues to the "extraordinary life" may elect to focus on surface markers. Learning, for example, that Influencers do not sleep much, they may attempt to train themselves to survive on just a few hours of rest a night. (This is actually what young Bill Clinton did!) Or noting that Makers tend to promote their own work, they may spend a large amount of time trying to garner publicity. At an extreme, a parent might even absent himself from the home because he had learned that many extraordinary individuals lose or lack a parent during critical years of childhood. Such examples reveal a confusion; extraordinariness does not come about simply because one has donned the garb of a Master or Maker.

The error of focusing on the surface characteristics of extra-ordinariness is conveyed amusingly in this testimony by Alfred Brendel, himself one of the extraordinary pianists of our era:

> I did not come from a musical or intellectual family. I am not Eastern European. I am not, as far as I know, Jewish. I have not been a child prodigy. I do not have a photographic memory; neither do I play faster than other people. I am not a good sight reader. I need eight hours' sleep. I do not cancel concerts on principle, only when I am really sick. My career was so slow and gradual that I feel something is either wrong with *me* or with almost anybody else in the profession. . . . Literature—reading and writing—as well as looking at art have taken up quite a bit of my time. When and how I should have learned all those pieces that I have played, besides being a less than perfect husband and father, I am at a loss to explain. [quoted in Alvarez, 1996, p. 49]

I am suspicious of programs that purport to train creativity or leadership—most notoriously, in a weekend workshop. To be sure, such experiences can alter one's attitudes toward one's own abilities or unleash some already developed talent that allows one to engage in (small *m*) making or (small *i*) influencing. But the extraordinary career is the result of experiences that can only unfold over years, even decades: there is no chance that the crucial components can be trained in a matter of days.

My studies suggest some lessons about milieus that are conducive to extraordinariness. The orderly bourgeois life—dull though it may seem—continues to have much to recommend it. It is advantageous for the young person to encounter adults who believe that one should work steadily in order to improve one's skills in one or more domains. Love and other forms of support are important, but it may be strategic—if not admirable—to link such affection to signs that the youngster is applying herself to a task and making steady progress within a domain.

Role models are crucial. Either directly or through some kind of symbolic object (books yesterday, films and television today, electronic networks tomorrow), the aspiring youth ought to be exposed to individuals who pursue their mission even when the going gets rough. Parents or coaches can help the youngster to deal with the inevitable disappointments and setbacks. While it is unrealistic to ignore a disappointment, there is a decisive difference between wallowing in momentary failures and exploiting them as prods, challenges, opportunities for a lesson.

The youth "at promise" as opposed to "at risk" needs to become acquainted with other individuals of talent and to sort out her mission in the milieu in which it is likely to be played out. Future Makers gravitate to cultural centers where they search for—and make common cause with—others of their breed. Of course, not all of those aspiring painters who move to New York City end up with canvases on display at the Whitney Museum; indeed, most of them will ultimately sell insurance or, if they are fortunate, teach visual art at high schools or arts academies. But only if they have the opportunity to become acquainted with the domain and the field of their time is there a chance that they will be selected out as special.

As domains become increasingly technical, it becomes far more difficult to make a mark in the absence of training. Future scientists, who might have succeeded with a bachelor's degree eighty years ago, now need at least one postdoctoral stint. Aspiring performing artists must spend time at Juilliard, working with a master teacher for many years. Only in the newest areas—for example, creation of software—is there opportunity for an individual who lacks established credentials. And yet there is a risk for the individual who remains forever in training. At a certain moment, she must test her wings and risk flying solo in an often hostile environment.

Factors relevant for the future Influencer are less well defined. The personal, linguistic, and existential skills that mark the effective storyteller are as likely to be mastered on the street as in the classroom. And the kind of life experience that leads to an authentic story that can be convincingly embodied is not, by definition, readily acquired by formal training. (To be sure, to the extent that one allows one's story to be fashioned by a "spinmaster," one sacrifices autonomy to formula. Such a course is unlikely to succeed over the long haul.)

Perhaps the most important formative experience for the future Influencer is the opportunity to challenge authority without being rejected totally. Such a challenge is most likely to succeed if the merits of the case are well founded and if the challenge is brought off with the proper blend of confidence and humility. Again, formulas seem implausible here; but it may well be important both to have observed role models who effect this kind of challenge and to have had local opportunities to practice measured defiance. Even Hitler had to negotiate countless barroom controversies before he could successfully defy better-known individuals who occupied official positions.

The future Maker need not challenge figures of authority directly. Yet she ultimately faces the same dilemma, because any breakthrough in a domain will ultimately alter the terrain of authority in that domain. In the manner of the indirect Influencer, a Maker like Virginia Woolf or Martha Graham challenges authority at one step removed, through the iconoclastic symbolic products that she has wrought.

Extraordinariness, then, is most likely to emerge if aspiring individuals are exposed to extraordinary models; ponder the lessons embodied in those models; and have the opportunity to enact critical practices in a relatively protected setting. Yet it is important to bear in mind that individuals become extraordinary in their own ways, and so each new Master, Maker, Influencer, or Introspector may have a unique saga to relate.

Three Key Elements: Reflecting, Leveraging, and Framing

My studies have called attention to three features that are regularly associated with extraordinary accomplishment—features, indeed, that interact with one another in a dynamic way. I will first introduce them as they are encountered in the lives of exemplary figures, and then turn to the ways in which they might be realized in more ordinary lives.

Reflecting

Having reached our adult years, and attained a certain level of competence in our chosen pursuits, we cannot assume that lessons from experience will automatically dawn on us. We are well advised to devote effort to understanding what has happened to us and what it means—what we are trying to achieve and whether we have succeeded. At a premium here is the activity called *reflecting*—regular, conscious consideration of the events of daily life, in the light of longer-term aspirations. Such reflection need not occur in journals or notebooks or, for that matter, even in the linguistic symbol system. Picasso kept almost two hundred notebooks over the course of his lengthy career, but there were very few words in the notebooks. Still, the regular habit of thinking in the relevant symbol systems stood him in good stead.

Consider, in this regard, our four model figures. From an early age, Freud was constantly involved in thinking about his aspirations and the success (or failures) that he was encountering along the way. His accounts of his case studies, and his analyses of his own dreams, served as indispensable aids in the advancing of his own thinking and, ultimately, his program of institution building. Virginia Woolf used conversation and written accounts to reflect on virtually every aspect of her existence; her combination of essays, diary, letters, and fiction constitutes an exemplary record of reflection.

Our other two cases offer equally powerful, though contrasting, accounts of reflection. Gandhi took daily walks, meditated on a daily basis, engaged in regular strategy sessions with his closest associates, and was forever immersed in the production of newspapers, books, and broadsides—including his own invented form of reflection about the challenges that he tackled daily: the "experiment with truth." Mozart showed a capacity for reflection in early childhood in the many letters he wrote to family members; often these letters included discussions of the musical problems and challenges that he was confronting, as well as amusing comments on the events of the day. In later years, there is less documentary evidence for reflection except, alas, about his difficulties with his father and his declining financial situation. But, instructively, when confronting musical challenges, as in his composition of the six Haydn quartets, Mozart not only left a written "score" of his struggles but also cited them pointedly in his dedication to the admired Haydn.

Just as one ought to reflect upon work, it is important to monitor one's potential audiences—be they family, friends or peers, or those unknowns who will ultimately render judgment about inventions or writings. Lessons from our exemplars are clear. Seek feedback and listen to what others are saying. Do not be overwhelmed; it is important not to jettison one's own critical faculties. But, especially during formative years, savor the careful feedback of individuals knowledgeable in the domain.

Reflecting is, by definition, conscious. Two other activities need not be explicit, but they are equally important; and they ultimately interact with reflection.

Leveraging

We are all deviants from the norm in one or more particulars—in the accidents of our birth, our combination of intelligences, the contours of our personality, the particular experiences that we undergo at home, in school, on the streets. Some of us have quite stunning deviations: Mozart was a musical adult in the body of a child; Freud was a Jew seeking recognition in anti-Semitic Vienna; Woolf was an androgynous woman, without formal education, who was writing a new chapter in English literature; and Gandhi was a provincial Indian who sought to change the policies of the most powerful empire of his time . . . and the thinking of the rest of the world.

But it is less the fact of asynchrony per se that distinguishes extraordinary individuals: crucial is the extent that they can identify this unusualness and make it work for them. In speaking of *leveraging*, I refer to the capacity of certain individuals to ignore areas of weakness and, in effect, to ask: "In which ways can I use my own strengths in order to gain a competitive advantage in the domain in which I have chosen to work?" The widely admired scientist and writer Stephen Jay Gould provides a paradigm case here. Lamenting that he is not strong in the areas of mathematics or logic, he explains:

> All people have oddly hypertrophied skills but some folks never identify their uniqueness properly. . . . I did receive one gift from nature's pre-eminent goddess, Fortune—a happy conjunction of my own hypertrophy with maximal utility in a central professional activity. I cannot forget or expunge any item that enters my head, and I can always find legitimate and unforced connections among the disparate details. In this sense I am an essay machine. [Gould, 1995, pp. xi–xii]

Each of our four figures approached leveraging in a characteristic way. For Mozart, no problem existed. A prodigy from the earliest years of his life, he simply pursued a musical career in the most serious and total sense. Freud's conundrum was challenging; he had to use his range of scholastic strengths (language, personal abilities) and limitations (spatial and logical reasoning) to constitute a scientific career. When not as successful as he would have wished in the domain of neurology, he cast about for an approach to psychology in which his own strengths in thinking and organization could grant him a comparative advantage over his contemporaries.

Virginia Woolf was similarly talented in the linguistic and personal domains, though her own genius was oriented toward introspection rather than influencing. Self-confident to a point, she was more fragile in the face of criticism than was Freud. By relying on written words and private conversations, while avoiding face-to-face public debates, she met others on her strongest ground.

Gandhi's deep explorations of his own psyche and that of the Indian people allowed him to create a form of protest that was ideally suited to the Indian struggle for independence. He did not worry about the fact that he had not been a good student or that he lacked the platform of a member of the establishment; instead, he insisted that all persons meet him as a fellow human being—thereby casting aside the biases of race, class, and ethnicity.

Identification of strengths yields an additional dividend. Frequently, breakthroughs occur because the individual has been able to conceive of familiar problems or challenges in a new way. Consider Freud in matters of the psyche (bringing considerations from the nursery to adult pathology); or Gandhi dealing with social conflict (melding the perspectives of Westerner and Eastener). Such reconceptualization is most likely to come about if an individual has *multiple representations* of a problem—that is, if he or she can think about the problem in a number of ways, particularly ways that have not previously been brought to bear on that problem. The more that an individual can make use of his unique strengths in attacking a problem, the more likely that he will arrive at an approach that holds special, hitherto unanticipated promise for illuminating that problem.

Framing

The capacity to identify one's deviance and to convert it into a competitive advantage exemplifies the third feature of extraordinariness, what I have termed framing. Briefly, *framing* is the capacity to construe experiences in a way that is positive, in a way that allows one to draw apt lessons and, thus freshly energized, to proceed with one's life.

Every day each individual encounters some experiences that go well and some that don't. The extraordinary individual is not out of touch with reality; she does not paint clear successes with the brush of failure, nor does she resort to Pollyannaish attempts to ignore a failure. Critical is the capacity to see not so much the bright side of a setback as the learning opportunity it offers—to be able to take what others might deem an experience to be forgotten as quickly as possible and instead to reflect on it, work it over, and discern which aspects might harbor hints about how to proceed differently in the future.

The cumulative effects of such framing should not be minimized. Suppose, conservatively, that a future creator or leader has one experience a week from which she learns an important lesson: a few hundred experiences will have accumulated within a few years. This accomplishment certainly places the individual in quite a different niche from the individual who does not pause to reflect or draw lessons at all, and from the individual who wholly misinterpets such experiences.

What may be inconsistent and inconstant for most of us becomes a *habit of life* for the extraordinary individuals. And while a deviation of ten or twenty experiences may not show up as a blip on a cumulative record, deviations of several hundred experiences mount up to genuine differences in how individuals lead their lives.

I have been struck by how, at every phase of his unusual career, Ronald Reagan was underestimated by most observers. Doubtless this was due to his easygoing personality, his tendency to engage in self-deprecation, and, perhaps, his lack of the analytic skills that one expects in top-flight Influencers.

Reagan was a Master at framing. Not only was he able to see the bright side of an apparent failure (indeed, he was perhaps a bit too prone to accentuate the positive); more important, he drew lessons from every one of his professional experiences, successful or not, and wove it into his experiences at the next post. The distance from the college sportscaster to the man in the Oval Office is enormous; but if one traces the steps from radio announcer to B-movie actor to president of The Screen Actors' Guild to pitchmaster for General Electric to candidate for high office in California, the seemingly enormous gap quickly becomes negotiable.

Let's consider our four individuals as exemplary framers. Following a childhood rich in opportunities and triumphs, Mozart faced one setback after another as an adult. Never did he deny these failures. However, he was determined to continue his composing; increasingly he became able to think of his life not in terms of the public reaction to his work but rather in the extent to which his works met his own exacting standards. Composing became a solace, not an occasion for stress.

In his struggle to find a scientific niche, and then to convince others of the power of his insights, Freud was also faced with constant frustrations. Rather than being crippled by such rejection, however, he came to accept it as par for the course. (Sometimes, indeed, he could account for such resistance in terms of his own theory.) Over the years, he devised an organizational base that allowed him to procced with his work on his own terms.

Virginia Woolf emerges as a partial exception to the framing hypothesis, since she could be intimidated by criticism and eventually made the decision to end her own life. She was not able to conquer the burden of manic-depressive disease. But over the course of her life, she became increasingly confident about her own abilities and increasingly dismissive of harsh criticism. Indeed, as we've seen, she came to see criticism as a stimulus to achievement—a textbook example of successful framing.

Finally, Mahatma Gandhi exhibited throughout his adult life a remarkable ability to absorb difficulties and criticisms and to put them to work in his behalf. Gandhi believed that there was a master plan for life and that those who pursued what was right would be touched with success. While inevitable, setbacks were not to be seen as disorienting. Not only was Gandhi able to frame events for himself in a positive way; he accomplished the more remarkable feat of convincing his followers that they, too, were triumphant even in moments of apparent defeat.

It may help to convey the importance of this trio of features if we consider what human potential would be like in their absence. To begin with, if an individual never engaged in reflection, she would be unlikely to learn from experience. Such a situation would be most maladaptive for someone bent on changing the world. If an individual did not try to leverage her skills to maximium advantage, she would find herself at a disadvantage in comparison to those who can play from strengths. Finally, if an individual were to accept every event as equally successful, or simply to internalize the interpretations and reactions of others, then she would be unlikely to embark on a course of distinctive achievement. It is the capacity to find meaning—and even uplift—in an apparently negative experience that fuels one to face life confidently and effectively.

The three features I've identified have close relations with one another. Reflecting is fundamental—the capacity to assume distance on oneself and one's experiences proves the sine qua non of effective accomplishment. That reflection typically proceeds in two directions: first, toward an examination of one's own strengths and liabilities; second, toward an examination of the lessons from daily experiences. Sometimes that examination is explicit, but sometimes it occurs implicitly, as a internalized habit of mind. Indeed, when one becomes conscious of one's own framing or leveraging, one is engaging in a reflective endeavor.

No individual can be in full control of his fate—our strengths come significantly from our history, our experiences largely from the vagaries of chance. But by seizing the opportunity to leverage and frame these experiences, we gain agency over them. And this heightened agency, in turn, places us in a stronger position to deal with future experiences, even as it may alter our own sense of strengths and possibilities.

Lessons for the Ordinary

Most of us will not achieve Making or Mastery with a capital M, Influencing or Introspecting with a capital I. Indeed, this is almost a logical necessity. In the absence of a captive audience or an appreciative set of judges, potentially extraordinary individuals would lack a playing field on which to try out their skills and leave a lasting imprint.

I have argued that what begins as relatively small deviations between the ordinary and the extraordinary can fan up more or less rapidly into distances that are clearly qualitative. It may be that at age one, a Beethoven or a Woolf, a Hitler or a Gandhi, are not that different from the rest of us; but at age twenty-five or fifty, the distance between "us" and "them" seems virtually unbridgeable. If the pianist Alfred Brendel began as someone indistinguishable from the rest of us, he had to accomplish many things to enter the ranks of the extraordinary.

Can we, the nonextraordinary, nonetheless derive lessons from these individuals—lessons that can have a meaningful impact upon our lives? I believe that the answer to this question is a firm yes. Principal lessons grow out of the four kinds of extraordinariness that I've identified and the three features that characterize a range of extraordinary individuals.

In our own lives, each of us will inevitably work in one or more domains. Through sustained effort, it is possible for normal individuals to master the key elements and levels of a domain. At the very least, we can operate at the level of the expert. But we face the choice of producing works of the highest quality in the domain, or of attempting to change the domain in ways that make sense to us. We cannot all revolutionize painting the way Picasso did, or cook in the manner of the chefs who created nouvelle cuisine. But we can each vary such domains in ways that bring pleasure to us and to those with whom we are in intimate contact.

Turning to the world of persons, the capacity to introspect deeply about oneself or to exert influence over others is part of the human condition. The options depend, first, on the willingness to devote years to pondering the world of human beings and, second, on the daring to embark on new paths. Again, we cannot all expect to achieve the introspective depth of a Woolf, or the influence over others of a Freud or a Gandhi. But in our more modest spheres, there is little question that insights about ourselves, or intuitions about others, can exert genuine and perhaps positive effects on those who are close to us.

Achieving success with one or more of these minds—our four extraordinary minds—depends significantly on the three features I have identified. If one hopes to make an impact on a recognized domain of work, or upon the world of individuals, one is well advised to engage in regular and searching introspective activities; to locate one's areas of strength and build upon them as much as possible; and, finally, to interpret daily as well as "peak" and "trough" experiences in ways that are revealing rather than defeating.

Of perennial importance is attention to excellence and high standards. Whether one seeks to change the world or to achieve a better quality of personal existence, one should always aim a bit higher. The Japanese speak of *kaizen:* the effort to improve a little each day. Even if the steps of improvement do not suffice to make one into a world figure, they will result in better performances and in a feeling of accomplishment. The social commentator John Gardner made this point memorably in his essay "Excellence": "The society which scorns excellence in plumbing because plumbing is a humble activity and tolerates shoddiness in philosophy because it is an exalted activity will have neither good plumbing nor good philosophy. Neither its pipes nor its theories will hold water" (1961, p. 86).

I am often asked, "How can I become extraordinary—a more powerful creator, a more successful leader?" Alas, there is not much one can do about one's biology, or, by the adult years, about one's intellectual strengths and one's personality. These can be tampered with only at the margins. But whether a poet or a plumber, one can learn a lot by studying the domain and by seeking to anticipate its trajectory. By the same token, one can benefit from understanding the existence, and the modes of operations, of relevant fields of judgment, whether they consist of twelve or twelve thousand people. In adult years, competitive advantage often accrues to those who "top off" their skills with nuanced appreciation of the operations of the domain and the field.

To the complementary question, "Will I be extraordinary?" I have a whimsical "bad news, good news" response. Because the field operates slowly, you may die without knowing that you are extraordinary. But because the field is so deliberate, you will also not know for sure that you are *not* extraordinary!

Faced with such interrogation, I make one more point. Discover your difference—the asynchrony with which you have been blessed or cursed—and make the most of it. Make your asynchronies fruitful, blissful. Take stock of your experiences—both those that you cherish and those that make you quake—and try to frame them in the most positive ways. *Positive* here does not necessarily mean self-congratulatory; rather, it means that you will try to understand what has happened or what you have done in a way that is most likely to work in your favor in the future.

In reviewing this list, I am aware that it contains few surprises—particularly to readers of this book. I note as well that there are candidate features that did not appear—for example, I have not stressed the importance of one's genes, one's religion, one's siblings, one's politics or ideology. I hope to have assembled a portrait of how a certain set of factors operate together in an individual over a significant period of time in order to yield, in the happiest instances, a life's work that makes a positive difference in our world.

Future Extraordinary Possibilities

Individuals have always attained extraordinariness in part by their capacity to use the artifacts around them. The first Maker to wield an ax or a sword laid claim to head his clan; eventually the Influencer who could command a battalion of well-armed men conquered his part of the world. Artists and scientists have always exploited the most recent innovations in their society; and while not all composers create electronic music and not all graphic artists utilize computer-aided design, future artists would be ill-advised to ignore these modes of communication. Indeed, according to the noted film director and producer George Lucas, movies no longer need to be made on location; they can be made as well within an electronic studio for a fraction of the cost (Lucas, 1995).

Yet, until now, it has remained clear that the human being is in charge. We are extraordinary because we design the computer programs and decide when to use them and when to pull the plug. If the time comes when the computer—in its many manifestations—is both posing and solving problems that are beyond human comprehension, then extraordinariness will increasingly reside in the world of artifacts. It remains to be seen whether those factors that remain distinctly nonartifactual— pain, vulnerability, a sense of finitude—will become more important or will also recede in significance.

An analogous shadow hangs over achievement when it is considered from a biological perspective. We rapidly approach the time when genetic engineering is likely to become a fact of daily life. Soon we will know which genes, or set of genes, are critical for certain cognitive capacities (high scholastic intelligence, musical talent, bodily skill) as well as certain personality combinations (bipolar disease, obsessiveness, perhaps even risk taking or skilled leveraging). If we choose to breed individuals on these bases, or engage in other forms of genetic engineering, then extraordinariness will again reside elsewhere—this time in the biological and engineering laboratories.

No one knows whether the specters I have described are unrealistic concerns, or whether they will descend upon us with frightening speed. I have little doubt, however, that if and when these possibilities become near certainties, the situation will wreak havoc on our long and still slowly evolving cultural institutions and traditions. It will require a rare breed of extraordinariness—melding Making and Influencing—to deal successfully with these unprecedented, difficult-to-fathom challenges.

No doubt individuals have always felt that certain events were outside their control; and throughout history, many persons have felt that events were moving too quickly for their own taste or temperament. There is little question that we live in a time when the rate and flavor of change are overwhelming. No one can fully anticipate the implications for our lives of high-speed computing, networking prospects, laser technology, the end of the cold war, the rise of global organizations, the new configurations of fundamentalism and tribalism—just to incant a few items from the front pages of every newspaper. As the columnist Jane Bryant Quinn recently quipped, "if you think you know what is going on, you haven't got a clue about what's going on."

This state of affairs has radical and troubling implications for human development in general and for the achievement of expertise in particular. Whatever the changes in earlier times, most individuals had reasonable confidence that they were raising their young for a world they themselves could envision. Until recently, even in modern secular society, the role of major professions (doctor, lawyer, accountant) and the blue-collar jobs (factory worker, household cleaner, hospital orderly) could be presumed to endure. One also assumed that the major institutions would remain (business workplace, factory, school, hospital, arts center) and that loyal workers in these institutions merited some semblance of job security.

All of this is now up for grabs. The role of doctor has changed more in the last twenty years than in the previous hundred. Computers and robots assume many of the roles that were once manned by ordinary individuals. Many of the most familiar institutions—like hospitals and the workplace—are changing so fundamentally that they may not be recognizable in future generations. Most troubling for much of the citizenry, there is effectively no job tenure anymore; individuals must expect to shift careers or at least positions throughout their lives. Nearly everyone lives with a Damoclean sword of structural unemployment or anachronistic skill hanging over his or her head.

Some welcome these changes, while many (including me) find them troubling. Clearly individuals differ from one another enormously in the extent to which they can handle challenges, risks, new opportunities. The gamut ranges from those who, according to Erich Fromm, wish to "escape from freedom" to those who, in Mihaly Csikszentmihalyi's term, undergo "flow" as they confront the unfamiliar and challenging. From the perspective of this study, it is the aspiring Makers—who seek the new, who are impatient or bored with the familiar—who are most "at promise" for achieving extraordinary feats. Conversely, those who are frightened or intimidated by the unknown are likely to wrap themselves in their expertise, hoping that it will suffice at least through their lifetime and that of their children.

But to draw an either/or dichotomy is too extreme. It may make more sense to think of all individuals as capable of *some* adventuring, particularly when the environment is friendly, and of all individuals as becoming overwhelmed by change when it courses forth too rapidly and unexpectedly. Where individuals differ from one another seems to be in their original threshold for change—which may be set by their genome; in their experiences, over the course of the early years of life, which either open them up to new experiences or make them increasingly suspicious and fearful of the unknown. Framing makes some difference here, but when framing becomes delusional, it is no longer functional.

Most of us are content to engage in what might be termed "little *e*" extraordinariness—perhaps dabbling in the writing of a poem or a story. Only a few individuals have the talent and the nerves to reach for the stars—to seek to attain "big *E*" Extraordinariness, where their contributions actually help to reconfigure a significant realm of human experience. These people may have to assume ever-increasing responsibilities in the brave new worlds to come.

Humane Extraordinariness

Taking a cue from our extraordinary mentors, I wish to frame this small work with an upbeat coda. Because of the variety of human beings who inhabit this earth, emanating from an enormous range of cultures, there are innumerable ways in which individuals can stand out and make a difference. Because of the finite capacities of our own minds, and because of the exigencies of communication, we tend to focus on just a few examples— and perhaps too often on the same examples: the Luthers, the Mozarts, the Grahams. In our own lives, all of us know unheralded individuals who make a difference in the quality of life. At the end of *Middlemarch*, George Eliot writes of her heroine Dorothea:

> The effect of her being on those around her was incalculably diffusive; for the growing good of the world is partly dependent on unhistoric acts; and that things are not so ill with you and me as they might have been is half owing to the number who lived faithfully a hidden life, and rest in unvisited tombs. [1962, p. 768]

Until this point in human history, we have had an enormous luxury—one we have exploited for only a few years and that we have now lost forever. That is the luxury of allowing our talents to develop freely and fully in whichever ways they can. The opportunity to do this has been hard-won, chiefly in the West and chiefly since the seventeenth century. Before that, individuals were not encouraged to distinguish themselves from the crowd, and those who did so were as frequently greeted with a death sentence as with a garland of flowers or a niche in the pantheon.

Many individuals, including readers of this book, have benefited from this almost accidental opportunity. And many of us, including me, are loath to give up the chance to allow our minds to operate freely, or to withhold this opportunity from others.

Yet, as the possibilities of destroying or radically remaking our world loom large, and as the civilization becomes increasingly global in most respects, we are confronted with an epochal dilemma. If we allow Making and Influencing to express themselves freely, without regard for consequence, we stand at high risk of a world destroyed (by a new weapon) or rendered uninhabitable (thanks to a genetic experiment run amok). If, on the other hand, like Sparta following Athens or the Nazis following Weimar, we instill severe measures to restrict such expression, we relinquish the very liberties for which so many individuals of goodwill have worked for many centuries.

Mihaly Csikszentmihalyi, William Damon, and I have coined a phrase to express a phenomenon we hope will prove adequate to this challenge. We call it *humane creativity*—a phrase I have reformulated for present purposes as *humane extraordinariness*. We argue that with the invaluable opportunity to use one's mind and resources freely, there should come a concomitant responsibility to use them well and humanely. We call not for censorship but rather for an ongoing serious grappling with the social, economic, political, and cultural implications of what one has made or how one has exerted influence. Operating either as individuals or as members of crafts and disciplines more corporately, those who have the opportunity to engage in extraordinary work ought to make exemplary efforts to use that work responsibly; similarly, such extraordinary people should share the rationale for their efforts with the public that supports them and that must live with the consequences. We cannot afford a situation of business as usual, where the onus for dealing with the fallout from a person's creation falls on "someone else." We cannot impute responsibility for the uses of our words, our works, our inventions to religions, the law courts, some other estate or community. Rather, such vigilance becomes the responsibility—though not the sole responsibility—of individuals who are graced with the opportunity of initiating exciting new lines of creation.

The seeds for humane extraordinariness exist. They exist in part in the guiding principles that have traditionally resided within artistic and professional domains: the Hippocratic oath for doctors, the truthfulness of the scholar, the dedication to justice of the lawyer, the disinterestedness of the guardian, in Plato's sense. Alas, these beliefs and practices have been obscured and dampened in recent years, because of seductively powerful messages about self-interest and the marketplace. But they have not yet been totally silenced, and perhaps they can be revivified.

Here the human dimension comes in. One can produce books about morality in the hundreds, and mandate courses about ethics for every individual; but unless individuals of talent and promise—indeed, unless *all* individuals—have the opportunity to encounter living exemplars of humane extraordinariness, they will neither take this option seriously nor know how to strive for it in their own lives. Thus it becomes crucial for those involved in education to identify those persons and those institutions that, often bucking the tide, constitute examples of thoughtful, reflecting Making and Influencing. The heroes of the past—George Washington, Niels Bohr, Martin Luther King, Jr., Dorothy Day—and the heroes of the present, both sung and unsung, must be studied and their means of influence understood and reconstituted so that they speak to the present milieu. Here resides the ultimate rationale for studying the extraordinary: they provide the most viable landmarks by which the individuals of the future—ordinary no less than extraordinary—can chart their lives.

Such study, such emulation, should not deny the problematic aspects of extraordinary individuals—the stories of Sigmund

Freud or Mahatma Gandhi or Thomas Edison or Marie Curie are inspiring in their broad outlines, but cautionary in their details. Humans may be like gods, but they are also and equally like other animals. Indeed, an excess regard of heroes inevitably leads to the disillusion that plagues the former idealist. But in the absence of such exemplars—however partial, however flawed—we cannot even begin to think about more humane forms of creativity, leadership, and spirituality. And so, despite my avowed aim of describing rather than prescribing, I hope that this book may inspire as well.

REFERENCES

Alvarez, A. (1996). The playful pianist. *The New Yorker*, April l, 1995, pp. 49–55.

Arnold, K. (1995). *Lines of Promise*. San Francisco: Jossey-Bass.

Astington, J. (1993). *The child's discovery of mind*. Cambridge: Harvard University Press.

Bamberger, J. (1982). Growing up prodigies: The mid-life crisis. In *Developmental approaches to giftedness*. Ed. D. H. Feldman. San Francisco: Jossey-Bass, pp. 265–79.

Banks, J. T. (Ed.) (1989). *The selected letters of Virginia Woolf*. New York: Harcourt Brace Jovanovich.

Bate, W. J. (1963). *John Keats*. Cambridge: Harvard University Press, pp. 260–61.

Bate, W. J. (1975). *Samuel Johnson*. New York: Harvest.

Bell, A. O. (Ed.) (1977, 1978, 1980, 1983, 1984). *The diary of Virginia Woolf*. Vols. 1–5. New York: Harcourt Brace Jovanovich.

Bell, Q. (1972). *Virginia Woolf: A biography*. 2 vols. New York: Harcourt Brace Jovanovich.

Blom, E. (Ed.) (1956). *Mozart's letters*. Harmondsworth, England: Pelican.

Bloom, B. (1985). *Developing talent in young people*. New York: Ballantine Books.

Bondurant, J. (1958). *Conquest of violence: The Gandhian philosophy of conflict*. Berkeley: University of California Press.

163

Bouchard, T. J., D. T. Lykken, M. McGue, N. L. Segal, and A. Tellegen. (1990). Source of human psychological differences: The Minnesota Study of Twins Reared Apart. *Science* 250, 223–28.

Brown, J. M. (1989). *Gandhi: Prisoner of hope.* New Haven: Yale University Press.

Clark, R. (1980). *Freud: The man and the cause.* New York: Random House.

Colby, A., and W. Damon. (1992). *Some do care.* New York: Free Press.

Coles, R. (1997). *Moral intelligence.* New York: Random House.

Csikszentmihalyi, M. (1990). *Flow.* New York: HarperCollins.

Csikszentmihalyi, M. (1996). *Creativity.* New York: HarperCollins.

Edel, L. (1978). *Henry James.* New York: Avon Books.

Einstein, A. (1945). *Mozart: His character, his work.* New York: Oxford University Press.

Eliot, G. (1962). *Middlemarch.* New York: Crowell-Collier.

Ericsson, A., R. T. Krampe, and C. Tesch-Romer. (1993). The role of deliberate practice in the acquisition of expert performance. *Psychological Review* 100 (3): 363–406.

Erikson, E. (1959). *Identity and the life cycle.* New York: International Universities Press.

Erikson, E. H. (1969). *Gandhi's truth.* New York: Norton.

Feldman, D. H. (1994). *Beyond universals in cognitive development.* Norwood, N.J.: Ablex.

Feldman, D. H. (with L. T. Goldsmith). (1986). *Nature's gambit.* New York: Basic Books.

Fischer, L. (1950). *The life of Mahatma Gandhi.* New York: Harper and Row.

Fischer, L. (1983). *The essential Gandhi.* New York: Vintage.

Freud, S. (1895). *Project for a scientific psychology.* In *The origins of psychoanalysis: Letters to Wilhelm Fliess, drafts, and notes, 1887–1902.* New York: Basic Books, 1954.

Freud, S. (1900). *The interpretation of dreams.* In *The basic writings of Sigmund Freud.* Ed. A. A. Brill. New York: Modern Library, 1938 ed.

Freud, S. (1958). *Creativity and the unconscious.* Ed. B. Nelson. New York: Harper and Row.

Freud, S. (1961). *Dostoevsky and Parricide.* In *The standard edition of the complete psychological works of Sigmund Freud.* Ed. J. Strachey. Vol. 21. London: Hogarth Press.

Fromm, E. (1941). *Escape from freedom.* New York: Rinehart.

Gandhi, M. (1948). *Autobiography: The story of my experiments with truth.* New York: Dover.

Gardner, H. (1983). *Frames of mind: The theory of multiple intelligences*. New York: Basic Books (second edition, 1993).

Gardner, H. (1991). *The unschooled mind: How children think, how schools should teach*. New York: Basic Books.

Gardner, H. (1993a). *Creating minds*. New York: Basic Books.

Gardner, H. (1993b). *The arts and human development*. New York: Basic Books.

Gardner, H. (1993c). *Multiple intelligences: The theory in practice*. New York: Basic Books.

Gardner, H. (1995). *Leading minds: An anatomy of leadership*. New York: Basic Books.

Gardner, H. (In press.) Extraordinary cognitive achievements. In *Handbook of child psychology*. Ed. W. Damon. Vol. 1, ed. R. Lerner. New York: Wiley.

Gardner, J. (1961). *Excellence*. New York: Harper.

Geschwind, N. (1977). Behavioral changes in temporal lobe epilepsy. *Archives of Neurology* 34: 453.

Geschwind, N., and A. M. Galaburda. (1987). *Cerebral lateralization*. Cambridge: MIT Press.

Goertzel, V., and M. G. Goertzel. (1962). *Cradles of eminence*. Boston: Little, Brown.

Gould, S. J. (1977). *Ontogeny and phylogeny*. Cambridge: Harvard University Press.

Gould, S. J. (1995). *Dinosaurs in a haystack*. New York: Harmony.

Grove's Dictionary of Music and Musicians. (1980). New York: St. Martin's Press.

Gruber, H. (1981). *Darwin on man*. Chicago: University of Chicago Press.

Gruber, H. (1982). Piaget's mission. *Social Research* 49, 239–64.

Herrnstein, R., and C. Murray. (1994). *The bell curve*. New York: Free Press.

Hildesheimer, W. (1982). *Mozart*. New York: Farrar Straus Giroux.

Hollingworth, L. (1942). *Children above IQ 180*. Yonkers, N.Y.: World Book.

Jamison, K. (1993). *Touched with fire: Manic repressive illness and the artistic temperament*. New York: Free Press.

Janik, A., and S. Toulmin. (1973). *Wittgenstein's Vienna*. New York: Touchstone Press.

Jones, E. (1961). *The life and work of Sigmund Freud*. Edited and abridged by Lionel Trilling and Steven Marcus. New York: Basic Books.

Kagan, J. (1994). *Galen's prophecy*. New York: Basic Books.

Kaufmann, W. (Ed.) (1980). *The portable Nietzsche*. New York: Viking.

King, J. (1995). *Virginia Woolf*. New York: Norton.

Lucas, G. Quoted in *New York Times*, Dec. 25, 1995.

Masson, J. M. (1985). *The complete letters of Sigmund Freud to Will-helm Fliess, 1887–1904*. Cambridge: Harvard University Press.

Mehta, V. (1976). *Mahatma Gandhi and his apostles*. New York: Viking.

Miller, L. L. (1989). *Musical savants: Exceptional skill in the mentally retarded*. Hillsdale, N.J.: L. Erlbaum.

Nanda, B. R. (1985). *Gandhi and his critics*. Dehli, India: Oxford University Press.

Nechita, A. (1996). *Outside the line*. Atlanta: Longstreet Publisher.

Payne, R. (1990). *The life and death of Mahatma Gandhi*. New York: Dutton.

Perner, J. (1991). *Understanding the representational mind*. Cambridge: MIT Press.

Piaget, J. (1983). Piaget's theory. In *Handbook of child psychology*. Ed. P. Mussen. Vol. 1. New York: Wiley.

Plomin, R., M. Owen, and P. McGuffin. (1994). The genetic basis of complex human behaviors. *Science* 264, 1733–39.

Policastro, E., and H. Gardner. (In press). From case studies to robust generalizations: An approach to the study of creativity. In *Handbook of creativity*. Ed. R. J. Sternberg. New York: Cambridge University Press.

Poole, R. (1990). *The unknown Virginia Woolf*. Atlantic Highlands, N.J.: Humanities Press International.

Robbins-Landon, H. R. (1988). What Haydn taught Mozart. *New York Times*, Aug. 19, 1988, sec. 2, p. 23.

Sacks, O. (1990). The twins. In *The man who mistook his wife for a hat*. New York: Harper Torchbook.

Sacks, O. (1995). *An anthropologist on Mars*. New York: Knopf.

Schonberg, H. (1969). It all came too easily for Camille Saint-Saëns. *New York Times*, Jan. 12, 1969, sec. 2, p. 17.

Selfe, L. (1977). *Nadia*. New York: Academic Press.

Shirer, W. L. (1979). *Gandhi: A memoir*. New York: Simon and Schuster.

Simons, J. (1990). *Diaries and journals of literary women from Fanny Burney to Virginia Woolf*. London: Macmillan.

Simonton, D. K. (1994). *Greatness: Who makes history and why*. New York: Guilford Press.

Solomon, M. (1995). *Mozart: A life*. New York: HarperCollins.

Sternberg, R. J. (1996). *Successful intelligence*. New York: Simon and Schuster.

Stevenson, H., and J. Stigler. (1994). *The learning gap*. New York: Simon and Schuster.

Storr, A. (1996). *Feet of clay*. New York: Free Press.

Sulloway, F. (1996). *Born to rebel*. New York: Pantheon.

Suzuki, S. (1969). *Nurtured by love*. New York: Exposition Press.

Terman, L. M. (1925). *Genetic studies of genius*. Vol. l: *Mental and physical traits of one thousand gifted children*. Stanford, Calif.: Stanford University Press.

Terman, L. M., and M. H. Oden. (1947). *Genetic studies of genius*. Vol. 4: *The gifted child grows up*. Stanford, Calif.: Stanford University Press.

Toulmin, S. (1978). The Mozart of psychology. *New York Review of Books* 25, 51–57.

Turnbull, C. (1972). *The mountain people*. New York: Simon and Schuster.

Turner, W. J. (1956). *Mozart: The man and his works*. Garden City, N.Y.: Doubleday Anchor.

Wellman, H. (1990). *The child's theory of mind*. Cambridge: MIT Press.

Weschler, L. (1990). *Shapinsky's karma, Boggs's bills, and other true life tales*. New York: Penguin.

White, M. (1987). *The Japanese educational challenge*. New York: Free Press.

White, S. (1965). Evidence for a hierarchical arrangement of learning processes. In *Advances in child development and behavior*. Ed. L. Lipsitt and C. Spiker. Vol. 2. New York: Academic Press.

Wilson, E. (1961). *The wound and the bow*. London: Methuen University paperbacks.

Winner, E. (1996). *Gifted children: Myths and realities*. New York: Basic Books.

Woolf, L. (1964). *Beginning again: An autobiography*. New York: Harcourt, Brace, and World.

Woolf, V. (1919). *Night and day*. London: Duckworth.

Woolf, V. (1925). *Mrs. Dalloway*. New York: Harcourt Brace.

Woolf, V. (1927). *To the lighthouse*. New York: Harcourt Brace and World.

Woolf, V. (1928). *Orlando*. New York: Harcourt Brace.

Woolf, V. (1929). *A room of one's own*. New York: Harcourt, Brace.

Woolf, V. (1931). *The waves*. Harmondsworth, England: Penguin.

Woolf, V. (1985). *Moments of being*. New York: Harcourt Brace.

⌐INDEX